516

JOHN BARBIROLLI

JOHN BARBIROLLI

A Biographical Sketch

JOHN BARBIROLLI

By

CHARLES RIGBY

With fifteen illustrations

ALTRINCHAM
JOHN SHERRATT AND SON

First published 1948

Made in Great Britain. Printed at the St Ann's Press
Timperley, Altrincham

PREFACE

To write a book about a person still living must always be a delicate business. The reasons are plain enough. In the present case the modest aim has been to achieve a tolerably objective portrait, largely in narrative form, of an international figure. In the course of a year probably not fewer than half a million people attend concerts all over Britain at which the Hallé Orchestra is conducted by John Barbirolli. I asked myself, what do these people know about the man with the baton, whose every look, every gesture, shapes the performance and makes it a thing worth remembering? Most of them really know but little about him. Yet as they sit there, watching and listening, many must wonder, and become filled with curiosity, albeit legitimate and respectful, about what manner of man he is, about his inmost nature, his growth and his past achievements.

Here, then, is the record, compiled for the most part from contemporary sources. It omits nothing, I hope, that might help the reader to form as complete a picture as possible of the famous man who has aroused his interest.

What I have tried to do is to present Barbirolli in all his aspects. And the best way to do so seemed to be to go to the newspapers and periodicals which have recorded his behaviour and his sayings down the years, a resource, incidentally, not unknown to writers who practise what is called the historical method. In this task I have been fortunate in having at my disposal a mass of Press cuttings, by whose aid I have been able to check and counter-check matter outside my own knowledge. I have tried to refrain from making any large claim for the subject of this book myself, preferring to leave that to the other people whose opinions and judgements I have quoted.

At the same time, within the limits of the material available, I have not neglected the other side of the argument. One well-known London critic once referred to Barbirolli as " Britain's greatest conductor ". That was a statement which it would be well-nigh impossible either to prove or disprove. As Shakespeare said: " greatness knows itself . . ." There is no yardstick. None the less, I make bold to think that there is greatness in the man, and greatness of a kind which is by no means common in the musical world. For Barbirolli himself, it has been enough that he should have done what he has done in dedicating his life to music. And for those who have watched his career and can in some degree assess his services to music, both in this country and the United States, comparison with contemporary conductors would neither add to his stature, nor take anything away from it.

Apart altogether from any question of greatness or present prestige, Barbirolli's has so far been an extraordinary career from whatever angle you regard it, and he can be said to be only half way through it. One of his most remarkable achievements was his success in America. A little more than ten years ago, when he was not yet thirty-seven, one of the biggest plums of the orchestral world was offered to him without any of his seeking—the conductorship of the New York Philharmonic Symphony Orchestra—and he was finally chosen to succeed Toscanini in that post. There could have been no stronger proof of his standing in the world of music at that time. Accustomed to the spectacular, and to exhibitionism of all kinds, the American public found in him a strange type of person. A man just appointed to direct their greatest orchestra, who could tell reporters at first sight, " I'm only a simple fellow ", was a new one on them. How he acquitted himself thereafter will appear later.

A good deal of emphasis has been placed on this phase of Barbirolli's career, because it is the least known in this country. If my book may seem to be wanting in some minor respect as a complete record, it has been partly due to one of Barbirolli's most engaging qualities—his personal modesty. For, once he consented, rather reluctantly, to provide such co-operation as was necessary, he was inclined to restrict it to what seemed to belong to history and to the public. It is my hope, however, that the result will be found worthy of the subject.

Sale,   CHARLES RIGBY
September 1948

ACKNOWLEDGEMENTS

To Mr. Barbirolli for the loan of Press cuttings and photographs; Mr. Philip Godlee and Mr. T. E. Bean, for looking over and correcting the Hallé chapters; Columbia Broadcasting System, U.S.A., for New York photographs; New York Philharmonic Symphony Society, for much material; *Picture Post* and Gerti Deutch for a photograph; Mr. John F. Russell, Librarian, Henry Watson Music Library, Manchester, for historical material on the Hallé Orchestra; and Mr. Joseph Barnes, secretary, Scottish Orchestra, for material about that orchestra.

CONTENTS

9

ILLUSTRATIONS

CHAPTER I

EARLY DAYS

THE Barbirollis on the father's side were a family of professional musicians from Italy who settled in London in the closing years of Queen Victoria's reign. On December 2, 1899, John Barbirolli was born at their home in the borough of Holborn, and christened Giovanni Battista. The family then occupied a suite of rooms over a baker's shop in Southampton Row, where Peters' Hotel and bar now stand. Mrs. Barbirolli was a native of the South of France. This blending of Italian and French strains—the perfect temperamental union for creative genius, combined with the true environment of Cockaigne—could hardly fail to produce at least one remarkable offspring, and it did. The Barbirollis enjoyed a happy, integrated family life, broken only by the storms and stress inevitable among a group of grown-ups and children whose whole existence centred around music. Besides John's parents, the household included grand-père Barbirolli, a violinist like Barbirolli's father.

Both father and grandfather had played in leading orchestras in Italy. They would recall with pride how they had played at La Scala, Milan, when Verdi's opera *Otello* received its first performance. They had also been playing in an orchestra at Brescia with a young musician named Arturo Toscanini, as Toscanini himself was to recall in 1930 when he brought the New York Philharmonic Orchestra to London. Memory was stirred in the maestro when John

Barbirolli was presented to him for the first time. Toscanini gazed at the young English conductor for a moment, drumming the table as he did so, as though trying to recapture a fleeting thought. Then, " Barbirolli," he asked, " are you not the son of Lorenzo, the violinist? " It must have been forty years since the Brescia days.

The Barbirollis had come to London in spite of reports spread about that England was not a musical country. They soon found that there was little truth in the reports, except that music in England was privately organized and not, as on the Continent, subsidized by the State. But they found also, at first, that for professional musicians individually, except those in the virtuoso class, life could be difficult enough.

In those days full-time professional orchestras whose players received yearly contracts and regularly weekly salaries were unknown in this country. And yet in London a competent player—and both the Barbirollis were that— might eke out a modest living if he was not particular whether he played in a symphony concert one night and in a theatre orchestra the next. That was the time when the " deputy system " was in force among orchestral players, a system which, while it was bad for the standards of performance, had the merit of providing employment to players who had not yet reached the leading desks. There were yet only one or two established orchestras in London, such as the Queen's Hall, and the London Symphony, which offered frequent engagements, and even these orchestras were apt to be different only in name.

It sometimes happened that the London Symphony Orchestra could not make up its strength from first-rate players available in London when a concert had been arranged, and Richter's Hallé Orchestra in Manchester had to be drawn upon to complete the complement. Often as

14

many as half the players came up from Manchester, and the London Symphony was all the better for their presence at a time when the Hallé, whether Londoners admitted it or not, was as good an orchestra as any playing in the Metropolis. London players like the Barbirollis relied chiefly on the orchestras of the big theatres for regular weekly engagements: theatres like the Empire and Alhambra in Leicester Square, which were for a long time the home of seasons of ballet, with Lydia Kyasht and Adeline Genee as star performers.

The Barbirollis were playing more or less regularly in the Empire Theatre orchestra. The famous " promenade " was still flourishing—an English compromise between a musical and a social occasion. " It's curious," Barbirolli says, " that Father spent his whole professional life in that triangle of the Victorian and Edwardian pleasureground—the Empire, Alhambra and Queen's Hotel." Later on, Lorenzo was to conduct Sunday evening " after dinner " orchestral concerts at the Queen's Hotel, in Leicester Square, a rendevous that retained a wide popularity, in the Edwardian spirit, up to recent years. There were regular performances by orchestras in both restaurant and grill room, and for Lorenzo's concerts the two would combine. It was at one of these concerts that John McCormack made his first appearance in London, as an unknown singer for a fee of one guinea.

This was part of the background for the awakening spirit of the boy John Barbirolli. It could be as stimulating as any in the world. Here the boy was at the very artistic core of the British Empire's capital. There was a constant procession of musical and theatrical events, about which he could read on the posters as he went to and from the Holborn Estate Grammar School. " As I walked down Kingsway," he says, " I saw the London Opera House built, almost stone by stone." The words " Conductor, HENRY

Wood," would appear often on the posters, and the name of Beerbohm Tree, the great actor-manager whose brother, Max Beerbohm, would now and then flurry the cultural life of London with his caricatures and exquisite literary ironies. There was Shaw at his best, the Shaw of *Fanny's First Play*, and Galsworthy and Arnold Bennett. But the boy's eye would perhaps dwell longest on the posters announcing Wood's Promenade Concerts, London's most popular musical event, then as now. Most dazzling of all were scenes at Covent Garden Opera House, near the Barbirollis' home, during the season.

Living in an atmosphere of music-making at home, and of endless musicians' shop, Barbirolli and his sister Rosie, without much persuasion, began handling any old violin that happened to be lying around. It seems to have been taken for granted in the family that, as the aptitude was inborn, both of them should be launched on a musical career, and that violin-playing should descend to the third generation. Both started with the violin. Rosie, born in 1895, later became a pianist. In 1911 a brother, Peter, was born. He in his turn took up the viola and is now playing in a London orchestra.

It was the old grandfather who saw the bright gleam in John, and because he had more spare time than Lorenzo, or more patience, he decided to take the boy's early musical education in hand. Grand-père Barbirolli was autocratic and uncompromising in his methods. He could scold fiercely, as well as praise loudly and warmly. He knew that music was a hard mistress. He also knew how prodigal she could be with her rewards to a persistent wooer. When the children were practising there would be a restless sort of exuberance in the Barbirolli home, with perhaps Mrs. Barbirolli looking into the room, smiling approval or gently protesting against the noise they were making.

16

EGERTON TIDMARSH (AT PIANO), WINIFRED SMALL
AND JOHN BARBIROLLI IN 1911

JOHN BARBIROLLI IN 1915

John himself has recalled those days. " We were living in a little place near Covent Garden," he said. " I was seven years old. Already I was playing the violin, but I was a fidget. I had to walk about as I practised. My grandfather was a bit of a fellow, and decided to stop this fidgeting and wandering around. So he bought me a 'cello, because, he said, I should have to sit down to practise, and not walk around as I was doing with the violin, and getting in everybody's way."

The 'cello was a good investment. John was forced to concentrate. He has never described himself at that age as a prodigy. But he made such good progress with the 'cello that five years later he was making his first public appearance, at Queen's Hall in a 'cello concerto with the Trinity College of Music orchestra. He went on to play all the classical 'cello concertos, and it was a revealing sight to see him conducting a year or two ago at Belle Vue, Manchester, on a Sunday afternoon, when Pau Casals played the Dvořák Concerto with the Hallé Orchestra. Barbirolli would turn occasionally to gaze with something like adoration at the Master, whose slightest performance is a memorable experience. And all the while, his mind would race back to that evening, thirty-four years before, when he himself sat playing a concerto in Queen's Hall as a boy of twelve. At a rehearsal Casals once turned to the orchestra, pointed to Barbirolli, and said, " Gentlemen, listen to him. He knows." If there was adoration on one side, at that Belle Vue concert there was deep respect on the other.

In the years just before the Kaiser's war musical prodigies were common enough, but they came mostly from abroad. The small boy that was Barbirolli created a stir in London musical circles. Even then he had developed a firm touch and an unerring feeling for the right phrase. But the boy himself learned one big lesson from the beginning—that

B   17

there was a vast amount of work to do before he could satisfy
either himself, or Grand-père Barbirolli, or Lorenzo. It was
then, too, as he watched Henry Wood, that the ambition
was born in him to become a conductor. That, however,
was a long way off. First work, and then more work. But
now, to the expert tuition from his grandfather and later
Herbert Walenn and others at the Royal Academy of Music,
was added the promise of success glimpsed on that night
from the platform of Queen's Hall. John worked hard, not
because he was made to, but because now he loved music
with his whole soul. Even then, there would be occasional
recitals in schools, the twelve-year-old Barbirolli being joined
by two other students at the academy for these—Winifred
Small (violin) and Egerton Tidmarsh, later professor at the
academy. And in between the hours of gruelling practice,
there would be frequent visits to Queen's Hall and the Royal
Albert Hall to worship at the shrine of such great visitors
as Paderewski, Kreisler, Pachmann, Kubelik; to hear the
swelling crescendos of the big orchestras under Wood or
Beecham, to hear the great operas at nearby Covent Garden
from the gallery.

Barbirolli regarded it as a sheer necessity to his musical
education to hear as many musical performances as possible,
even if it meant doing it cheaply, and at much inconveni-
ence. For, apart from concentrating intensely on mastering
the 'cello, at home or at the academy, the young Barbirolli
was already noting the technical aspects of public performances, the beat of the conductor, problems of timing and
tempo, and of ensemble playing generally. He tried to
discover how much the excellence of any performance was
due to the players in an orchestra and how much to the
conductor. He could form his own ideas on these questions,
but it was not until he himself held a baton in his hand
that all the answers came to him.

He certainly did not confine his studies to the music for his own instrument, but while still in his teens he would read all the musical scores he found at home and any others he could get hold of with the same thrilled interest as he read his favourite literary authors: Dickens, Thackeray, and Jane Austen.

It was then that the foundations of the catholicity of his musical taste were laid. He was interested in all great music, just as he was interested in most things outside the still esoteric world of music. Straight from his 'cello practice he would go to help his mother in her housework. He would even try a little cooking, and ever since then the cooking-stove has had an irresistible fascination for him. Even here he has contrived to be an artist; to cook a perfect meal has always been to him a matter of fundamental importance.

Barbirolli never knew the dream world of the musical amateur and concert-goer. He was too close to the mechanics of the thing, to the bitter disappointments and frustration that often came into a life devoted to music, not to know that it needed a good deal of strength of character and self-denial to fight the withering effects of disillusionment. The more he saw of orchestral players away from the concert hall, the more he realized that the scourges of the musical life must be accepted in a Job-like spirit. Triumph seemed separated from tragedy by the thinnest of screens. There could be no letting-up in the grip a musician had on himself. The more a musican put into his music, and the less into his private life, the more certain he was to achieve success and retain it. And Barbirolli meant to succeed, not for the sake of success, but because in a spirit of meekness and of gratitude to his Maker he felt that it was his life-work. This meekness and this gratitude have remained with Barbirolli ever since, as well as an endless wonder at the overflowing abundance of God's gifts to men. He has always seen a little farther into the heart of music than most of his contemporaries just because of that humility in his approach to the threshold. " The meek shall inherit the earth." Each day in his young life was a " new day big with promise ". He at least would not go the way of so many professional musicians and let the iron enter into his soul because of rebuffs and all manner of discouragement. Consequently the rebuffs for him were fewer, the discouragement easier to thrust aside.

For years he was to know opposition to the inevitable unfolding of his career in high musical places. Young rising musicians were too often looked upon as presumptuous interlopers. Barbirolli was to experience all this, often in an insidious and virulent form, but it did not deter him. His sense of vocation was too strong, his character too tough, to be put off by what others thought of him or by their efforts to keep him outside privileged circles.

In some notes on his early life which Barbirolli himself jotted down for inclusion in this book, he says: " It was in Goltermann's Concerto in A minor that I played at the Queen's Hall when I was twelve; the occasion was the orchestral concert of the Trinity College of Music, London, at which I was a student. The orchestra numbered nearly one hundred and was conducted by a Herr Wilhelm Sachse. The concerto itself was an extremely difficult virtuoso type of work now out of fashion and comparable perhaps to the violin concertos of Vieuxtemps. My father, to whose wisdom and great natural taste I owe so much, did one splendid thing for me. Even if I was not old enough to appreciate them fully, he took me early to hear all the great artists. So I can now say that I heard Saint Saëns play, and Ysaye and Pugnot give their famous Beethoven recitals. I also heard Santley sing.

" I had a passion for roaming round London. When

about eleven or twelve, I discovered the beauty of such sights as the Temple and the Little Cloister at Westminster Abbey. We always had a comfortable home, although never very wealthy, and always managed to spend two weeks at the seaside in summer—usually at Brighton, which I still adore. One great success I remember—but this came when I was sixteen—was when Ethel Bartlett (Rae Robertson had not yet come on the scene) and I gave a series of recitals of modern classical sonatas for piano and 'cello from memory —a thing almost unknown at that time. Ethel and I were among the earliest interpreters of the then new works of Goossens, Debussy, Delius, Ireland, Bax, and others."

Far from being possessed of transcendental feelings, or being in a state of permanent artistic exaltation, the young Barbirolli had a boundless curiosity about life. The bustle of the streets and pavements, the glitter of shop windows, the stream of London's traffic, were things that always fascinated him. Later on in his teens, what went on at Lord's cricket ground, or the Oval, would for the moment seem almost as important as what went on at Queen's Hall. Many of the things to which a boy's fancy leads him were denied him because of the family's meagre resources. Yet Barbirolli was already artist enough to accept music as rich compensation for the lack of the more material things. He found his greatest pleasure in simple pastimes. He studied London as methodically as he was studying Mozart. He became more of a Londoner than the Londoners.

So the years went on, with Barbirolli throwing himself into play with the same intensity as he did when he had his 'cello between his knees. His teachers were impressed by his extraordinarily keen intelligence. He could not only see farther into things, but see them more quickly than most youths of his own age. His musical intelligence and memory were already becoming marked.

About the time of Barbirolli's performance at Queen's Hall, and for a year or two afterwards, there seemed nothing likely to threaten the smooth course of London's life. Germany was causing anxiety from time to time, and there was much loose talk of war. But nobody believed that even if war came the life of the people would be torn up by its roots. But war did come, and life was torn up by its roots. During its early stages Barbirolli kept hard at his studies, although with one eye over his shoulder, looking at the war with a strange, restless excitement inside him that had nothing to do with music. He had been for nearly a year playing in Henry Wood's Queen's Hall Orchestra, when, at the age of seventeen, he joined the Suffolk Regiment. The war had only a year to run.

CHAPTER II

STRING ORCHESTRA AND OPERA

THERE is little to tell of Barbirolli's year in the army. He was proud to be in it, because he always liked the feeling of being in the stream of things. He chafed at the drill, only because he wanted to get to the front. But before he could get there the war was over. And so, back to music, a little more grown-up, physically fit, his sense of his musical destiny unclouded. He was faced with the problem of making a living, but he had the advantage of starting out with his technical equipment already above the average.

In England music had not suffered from the war as much as had been feared. As in Hitler's war, thousands of people, young as well as old, had turned to it for comfort and escape amid the ruin of their world. But it took some time before things found something like their normal level. The London of 1918–19 and that of 1913–14 belonged to two different epochs. But—music had survived, as it had survived other wars. Now people brought to it a deeper spiritual understanding born of years of suffering. Not only that, but the sense of release favoured a quick recovery in the world of art, in enterprise, an eager response among the musical public.

The young Barbirolli, although afire with ambition and full of confidence in himself, found the going hard during the first few years. He had to launch himself as a 'cellist and searched long for an opening for his considerable talent, backed by strong individuality. He played in London

23

cinema orchestras, hotels, at symphony concerts, and operas
—anywhere, so long, he says, " as I could go on working
independently ". He stresses this struggle to preserve his
" independence " of action, because he turned down many
an offer of help. He neglected no other opportunity to perfect his instrumental technique. This was one of the many
testing periods through which he was to pass before he rose
to his full stature. He never lost sight of the goal he had
set for himself, always pitched a little beyond his reach.
Drudgery was no more to him than a spur to rise above it.

His fibre withstood every attack of circumstance. His
musical sensibilities were, if anything, heightened by the
fact that all around him he heard slipshod performances by
musicians who had lost their first careless rapture, and who
played with a sort of cynical boredom, content just to earn
their pay—or their pint. He knew his hour would come.
While waiting for it, he was sustained by his zest for life,
his intense curiosity about all that went on around him.
Year by year his vitality increased.

In time he found his wings. By 1924 he had formed his
Barbirolli String Orchestra of twelve players. He also
became a member of a string quartet that broadened his
experience and enabled him to travel and see more of the
world. With his chamber orchestra, Barbirolli gave a series
of concerts at the Chenil Galleries, in Chelsea. It was
characteristic of him to choose this small medium to
habituate himself to the art of conducting and musical
interpretation. It was never likely to bring a spectacular
success in itself, but the performances were sufficient to
convince London music critics that here was a young conductor who knew what he was about; knew where he was
going and towards what goal.

The concerts met a need of the time. They were things
of quality and introduced to the public minor musical gems

by the classical composers. From the point of view of a livelihood, for Barbirolli they were not important, but in the making of him as a conductor they served their purpose. This was soon evident, for among those who attended the concerts of his chamber orchestra was Frederic Austin, head of the British National Opera Company, and Austin promptly engaged Barbirolli to conduct a series of opera performances.

Within a year Barbirolli was conducting at Covent Garden. " I think," he has said, " I was one of the few conductors at Covent Garden who did opera in four languages—English, French, Italian, and German." He first conducted the British National Opera Company, at Newcastle-on-Tyne, in Gounod's *Romeo and Juliet*, *Madame Butterfly*, and *Aïda*, all in one week. He had never before conducted an orchestra of more than twelve players, and never a chorus.

In 1930 Barbirolli was appointed Musical Director and Chief Conductor of the newly-formed Covent Garden Opera Company. He was then thirty. For three years he remained at Covent Garden, until he was appointed permanent conductor of the old-established Scottish Orchestra in Glasgow.

Barbirolli's promotion from the B.N.O.C. orchestra to conductor at twenty-five was a surprise only to those who did not realize that he had been making music in public in London and on the Continent for nearly ten years. Of his rehearsal, in *Trovatore*, with the orchestra, he says: " I called for a rehearsal of strings alone. ' The boy must have lost his head,' muttered some of my more experienced colleagues. But after three hours, devoted entirely to the first scene, they seemed to accept my own conviction. That was, that the accompaniments of Verdi, even in his early works, are packed with dramatic meaning, and only a careful study of their potentialities will suffice to expose the composer's intention.

"It is not a case of Oom-pah oom-pah! of standardized routine, but a suggestive background for the action on the stage." Thus, when his hour came, Barbirolli's continual and varied studies had borne fruit in positive, and what seemed to many, unorthodox ideas about the needs of performance.

By 1927 Barbirolli was conducting such diverse operas as *Romeo, Gianni Schicchi,* and *Rosenkavalier* at Covent Garden. "I realized," he says, "that even the intricacies of modern German opera made no demands more exacting than the ensembles of Verdi." To master these ensembles, he says, he had spent six months with the singers of *Falstaff.*

Barbirolli in winter toured the provincial cities with the Covent Garden Opera Company, after a three-month rehearsal period. For this tour some of the lesser artists of the International Summer Season were promoted to leading roles. English translations of the operatic texts were used, with libretti adapted by Professor Edward Dent, of Cambridge, and Proctor-Gregg, of Manchester. The company re-studied the words and music together. On this Barbirolli says: "Speaking as an Englishman, of Italian parentage and taste, I came to the conclusion that in opera especially the English language is indispensable for English audiences. Otherwise how can the textual allusions reproduced in the orchestra be appreciated? The subtlety of *Falstaff,* the brilliant humour of the *Barber of Seville,* can emerge only when the audience grasps the full meaning of the words." He goes on to say: "Even at La Scala, foreign opera is presented in the language of the audience. As far as I know, Debussy's untranslatable *Pelleas and Melisande* is the only work which has not been offered in Milan in Italian.

Generally speaking, if an opera is worth performing at all, the composer has reproduced in sound the meaning of the words; and when the sound alone is intelligible, half the meaning is lost." Later, at Covent Garden, Barbirolli conducted performances in which several of the stars of the New York Metropolitan Opera House appeared—notably Lawrence Tibbett's London début in *Tosca*, and Martinellis Calaf in *Turandot*.

" My experience with such artists," he says—and he has been associated with the world's finest—" is that the greatest of them are the first to ask for as many rehearsals as possible. They arrive at the time set and work till the very last moment. The ease which they gain from this preparation is of the greatest value to them." That fact—the ease in performance given by gruelling rehearsal—has been Barbirolli's guiding principle.

Moreover, he looks back on this operatic training as having been indispensable. It has made him a conductor of infinite resource and versatility. He believes that every conductor should begin that way. " The work is more difficult," he says. " There are more technical elements to master, and there are infinite last-minute emergencies and variations to deal with, which are a searching test of one's musical equipment and conducting technique. An entrance may be changed, a flicker of temperament may introduce some new situation. A musician whose instrument is lodged in his throat must necessarily be handled with infinite precision and delicacy. There are changes of mood and intensity. It is an absorbing business, this fusion of the multifarious elements that go to make up an operatic performance, and one which any conductor should cherish."

Barbirolli has shown throughout his subsequent career how a conductor can plan his symphonic programme from his experience in opera. Ten years after he was conducting

at Covent Garden he was thrilling New York audiences at
Carnegie Hall with the preludes and entr'actes from
Debussy's *Pelleas*—a work he knows by heart and will sing
through in French to anybody who will listen. He also performed in New York the entire first act of *Parsifal* with vocal
soloists. Carnegie Hall heard too, for the first time, the
entire second act of *Tristan* in the original uncut version.
And on that occasion, Kirsten Flagstad herself sang in that
version for the first time.

In 1927 " Signor " John Barbirolli, as one London newspaper called him, was both producer and conductor in what
he called " experiment " in running " off-season " opera at
Hammersmith and Wimbledon. " He is brimful of new
ideas and quite unafraid of putting them to the test," said
the *Daily Express* of this venture. Barbirolli himself told
how the thing came about: " I was giving a recital at the
Violoncello Club in June," he said. " Mr. Mulholland, who
owns the [King's] Hammersmith and Wimbledon Theatres,
was there. It suddenly struck me that he had his theatres
empty at this time of year. I suggested he might consider
the possibility of my producing *The Barber*, which has been
exceedingly successful on the B.N.O.C. tour. I spoke to him
on a Saturday and by the following Monday it was all
arranged.

" The B.N.O.C. gave me permission to present the opera
and provided the artists and the orchestra. The little experiment has paid. The enthusiasm of everybody over the pre-
sentation of *The Barber* at Hammersmith, right in the
middle of the dull season for such presentations, makes me
feel most hopeful for the future of opera."

Equally enthusiastic over the " experiment " was the late
J. A. Forsyth, critic of the *Daily News*. He wrote: " The
secret of opera finance has been solved. For years I have
argued, always to deaf ears, that the repertoire of opera com-

panies is too big, the expenses too big, and theatres too small. At last an enterprising impresario, Mr. Mulholland, of the King's, Hammersmith and Wimbledon, has chanced a fortnight's run of Rossini's *Barber of Seville* and much to his amazement has made money from the venture. That there is a large public for opera has been proved by Beecham and others, but the bottom of the purse has come. Every night, both at Hammersmith and Wimbledon, the theatres have been crowded. The performance, conducted by John Barbirolli, could not have been better. The cast, too, was exemplary: Miss Miriam Licette, Radford, Heming, Dennis Noble, and Heddle Nash being the principals. Unless I am mistaken, more will come of this." More, however, did not come of it, for Barbirolli soon had other work to absorb his energy.

And so, from opera, Barbirolli passed to purely orchestral conducting. He had already conducted the London Symphony Orchestra—then London's second oldest orchestra. And that represented about all the scope there was in London for his rapidly maturing gifts as an orchestral conductor. Wood and Beecham were so well-established that they had almost a vested interest in the major seasonal events. Malcolm Sargent had managed to secure a niche for himself with the Courtauld-Sargent series and the Robert Mayer Children's Concerts at the Central Hall. The B.B.C. Orchestra had only recently been formed, with its conductor in the position of something like a civil servant, red tape and all. A few years after its formation one of the governors of the B.B.C. suggested that the orchestra might conceivably benefit from playing under the more gifted younger conductors. The name of Barbirolli was mentioned. The reply was:

"Yes, we have in mind the question of giving one or two of our younger conductors a chance to conduct the orchestra. We propose to allow Leslie Heward to conduct a concert this year. Next year young Barbirolli will be given a trial."

But when next year came Barbirolli had already been appointed as Toscanini's successor in New York.

In those last years in the London he loved, Barbirolli was much in demand for gramophone recording. And it was here that his reputation as a conductor was established far beyond the shores of his native country. These engagements were profitable in every sense. They provided him with valuable conducting experience, and, even more important for his future, they brought him in contact with many great solo artists like Heifetz and Kreisler, who talked about the young conductor in American musical circles. Not only that, but his recordings were acclaimed by music critics all over the world as having great distinction. In preparing the orchestra for these invisible performances, he gave everything he had, for in recording—where there is no place for any kind of showmanship or the influence a conductor's personality and mannerisms have on an audience—it is the quality of the interpretation alone that counts. By that test Barbirolli's recordings stood and will continue to stand as long as the records are played.

Even the more familiar classics took on in his hands a new vitality, and all his recorded performances bear the marks of intensive preparation, and of minute attention to detail and nuance. The recordings began to be talked about, and there was the evidence of the gramophone companies that the name Barbirolli on a record was sure to make it something like a best-seller. Meanwhile Barbirolli's stock as a conductor was beginning to rise even in his own country. There was no orchestra in London with which he could become permanently identified to the exclusion of other conductors, but there were managements in the great cities of the North who were awaiting an opportunity of using his services.

His name rolled off the tongue beautifully and although it was an Italian name, there was the notion in most people's minds that the bearer of it was, as one New Yorker said some years later, " as British as a mutton chop or cricket ".

CHAPTER III

GLASGOW AND THE SCOTTISH ORCHESTRA

The first call came from Glasgow, from the management of the Scottish Orchestra. Little known outside Scotland, this orchestra had a history going back nearly a century. It had had a line of famous conductors in the past, including von Bülow, Sir Arthur Sullivan, Augustus Manns, Sir George Henschel and Sir Frederick Cowen. Manns conducted the orchestra for fourteen years, Cowen for ten. For many years it was, apart from the Hallé, the only established orchestra outside London carrying out a regular annual season, and if it had not existed Scotland would have heard no orchestral music at all, for those were the days when London orchestras seldom, if ever, went far afield.

That was one thing in favour of the continued existence of the orchestra. Like every other orchestra it had its ups and downs, but it has never lacked generous friends, who have dipped deeply into their pockets year after year to keep it going. Since the 1914–18 war there have only been one or two years when no call on the guarantors has been necessary. Private donations apart, the Glasgow Corporation between 1920 and 1944 paid out £40,590 towards the upkeep of the orchestra. And in 1943 the city voted an outright gift of £5,000 a year. During the last few years a movement, begun in Barbirolli's time with the orchestra (1933–36), to embrace other towns as financial contributors, has been greatly extended under Joseph Barnes, the energetic secretary, so that the Scottish

AT THE AGE OF 30, WHEN CONDUCTOR OF THE
COVENT GARDEN OPERA COMPANY

Orchestra has become more and more a national orchestra for Scotland.

The original organization out of which the present Choral and Orchestral Union of Glasgow (the society administering the Scottish Orchestra) eventually sprung was " formed for the purpose of trying out Handel's *Messiah* on a scale worthy of the greatness of the work ". Choral and orchestral elements were got together, and the performance took place on April 2, 1844, in the City Hall at Glasgow. The performance was a success, in spite of the fact that a local newspaper declared that it was a " blasphemous outrage on the sacred truths of the Scriptures ". Thirty years later the orchestra had thirty players and thereafter its strength fluctuated between fifty and ninety players. In the early years the season lasted for twelve weeks, and sometimes for sixteen. It was during the season of 1873 that von Bülow was engaged as conductor. At one concert he played the solo part in Beethoven's " Emperor " Piano Concerto as well as conducting the orchestra. He had taken Sullivan's place, but when the 1878 season came round the Berlin musical authorities forbade him to continue the engagement. The fine St. Andrew's Hall, seating 3,000 people, was opened in 1877, and during that season the orchestra made a profit which, however, was not repeated because of the expansion of the orchestra and the extension of the season. Julius Tausch, Schumann's successor at the Düsseldorf Conservatoire, took over the baton for the 1878 season, and in 1879 handed over to Augustus Manns, who had Cowen for some years as his assistant, until Cowen himself became permanent conductor-in-chief. Emil Mlynarski, the Pole, followed Cowen in 1911, but in 1914 the concerts were suspended for the duration of the Kaiser's war. For some years after the war had ended the orchestra had no regular musical director, though it had as guest conductors Koussevitsky,

Weingartner, Coates, Landon Ronald, Malko and others, all of whom thought highly of its capabilities.

Barbirolli was engaged to conduct the Scottish Orchestra for the 1933–34 season and subsequently. At the same time he conducted at occasional concerts of the Northern Philharmonic Orchestra in Leeds, then and since an unknown quantity, and now superseded largely by the new full-time professional Yorkshire Symphony Orchestra. When Barbirolli arrived in Glasgow the Scottish Orchestra was going through one of those periods of the doldrums which had occurred more than once in its history. It needed some powerful impulse to restore it to popular esteem, and some continuity in its direction. For Barbirolli it was his first permanent engagement as a symphony orchestra conductor. Great expectations were aroused on both sides by Barbirolli's acceptance of the post, and they were fulfilled, even if there was a feeling among many of the conductor's new following that the appointment was, perhaps, but another step on the road to his final destiny.

The fatal drawback of Glasgow in the eyes of a musician in process of acquiring an international reputation was its isolation from the main stream of Britain's music. This was, and must remain, a drawback that weighs heavily not only with potential conductors, but also with orchestral players. In the days when players were a floating population, moving about the country to towns which needed their services, this did not matter so much as it does nowadays, when the best players gravitate towards those orchestras which can give them all-the-year-round contracts or engagements. Scotland, however, has always produced enough competent players to reduce this handicap to manageable dimensions. Barbirolli, with sensational successes in London behind him, lost himself, as usual, in the task now ahead. He saw the orchestra was not in such good shape as it might be and set about putting it in order. In this he had the advantage of having plenty of enthusiastic support ready at hand, a body of private citizens as well as an enlightened city corporation, who would stick at nothing to get the best orchestra possible in the circumstances.

Barbirolli once called himself " something of a musical corpse-reviver," and it may be he regarded the Scottish Orchestra as a corpse, albeit a corpse capable of revival to a condition of some vitality. The Scottish Orchestra, at all events, revived under his touch and revived quickly. And among the players—and not in particular need of resurrection—was Evelyn Rothwell, at the first oboe desk. A few years later Evelyn was to become Barbirolli's second wife and a most charming and efficient helpmeet.

For three seasons Barbirolli took the Scottish Orchestra along with him, treading old and tired paths in the way of programme material and along paths new to Scottish audiences. All seemed set for a long and successful chapter in the life of the orchestra, when Toscanini resigned as musical director of the New York Philharmonic Orchestra. This event had first seemed to hold no particular significance either for the Scottish Orchestra or for Barbirolli. The 1935–36 season was drawing to a close and merely as a matter of professional curiosity Barbirolli, like everybody else in the musical world, would wonder who would lead the great American orchestra the following season.

First the New York orchestra's management sent an invitation to Wilhelm Fürtwangler, in Berlin, to fill the vacant post, and Germany's leading conductor had virtually accepted, but the offer had to be withdrawn in face of a storm of protest throughout America, a storm caused by the anti-Nazism then sweeping the United States. But although Fürtwangler was out of the running there were several eminent conductors in America who were known to be eager to assume Toscanini's mantle, and their chances were widely canvassed in the Press from the eastern seaboard to California. Barbirolli had gone to Holland to conduct, had forgotten that there was such an orchestra as the New York Philharmonic or that there was a job for a conductor. In any case, he knew that, except among a few influential musicians, he was unknown in America, and he had never set foot in the country in his life. Then came the staggering cable from Arthur Judson, manager of the New York Orchestra, asking whether he, Barbirolli, would accept a tentative engagement, which meant sharing the 1936–37 season with several other conductors, including Stravinsky and Rodzinsky. There had been no preliminary contacts between New York and the young Englishman before the cable came, and no one was more surprised than he was.

Barbirolli did not hesitate about accepting, subject to obtaining the necessary temporary release from the Scottish Orchestra. The news was received in Glasgow with emotion. " Of course, we will not stand in your way," they told him sadly. And yet the disappointment was offset by the feeling that the invitation from New York in a sense reflected honour on the Scottish Orchestra as well as on Barbirolli. A few months later Barbirolli was on his way to New York, to take up the " tentative " engagement which was to become permanent, or as permanent as such engagements can be. At the time it seemed to most of his friends that this appointment was the thing for which all that had gone before was but the preparation.

In the British Press it was made the occasion of a good deal of heart searching. There had previously been a danger of Henry Wood going to America. Now America had successfully lured the most outstanding of Britain's younger conductors, for whom apparently Britain could offer little inducement to stay. One London newspaper devoted a leading article to Barbirolli's departure It went something like this: " Here is one of Britain's most brilliant conductors leaving his native country because no one wanted him. It has been left to America to discover his gifts and to honour him as he should be honoured. Why did Britain let him go? Have we so many great conductors that one would not be missed? We must do something even now to keep Barbirolli among us, to use his great talents for the benefit of music in his native country." The writer of this article, being that most parochial of Londoners, a Fleet Street journalist, had evidently never heard of the Scottish Orchestra or of Barbirolli's magnificent work up in Glasgow. Evidently someone in New York had.

So, off Barbirolli went to New York, a tough little man who was to make that sophisticated capital sit up and forget that it had ever asked, " Who is this man Barbirolli? " But on his way over, the thirty-six-year-old Englishman did not feel especially tough. He had no illusions about what was in store for him.

CHAPTER IV

SUMMONS TO NEW YORK

BARBIROLLI crossed the Atlantic in the Cunard-White Star liner *Aquitania* and arrived in New York on October 27, 1936. His engagement was to conduct the Philharmonic Symphony Orchestra for the first ten weeks of the season beginning at Carnegie Hall on November 5th. Six other conductors were to share the remaining—and shorter—period between them. They included Igor Stravinsky, better known as a composer, Georges Ernesco, and Artur Rodzinski, who in his turn was to succeed Barbirolli at Carnegie Hall in 1943. It was understood that a final choice would be made from this septet in the course of the season.

Before Barbirolli arrived the American Press had had some weeks in which to discuss his appointment, regarded by most newspapers as sensational. The Press did its job with its usual thoroughness, sparing no detail, lacking nothing in candour. It focused on the young Englishman its great searchlights, and turned its army of reporters loose on him with a merciless barrage of questions. Because Barbirolli was almost unknown to the American public, his figure and personality had to be built up in the public's mind. While the New York newspapers generally showed good will, tinged with polite " sympathy " for the young conductor, a few of them took leave to doubt his prospects of success in what was perhaps the most difficult conducting job in the whole world. The unbelievers usually ended by saying, ". . . and of course, he is very young," the phrase that so often had gone against him at home.

In the wordy argument—and millions of words were spilled—one thing that seemed to the New Yorkers to need explanation to a metropolitan public was why Barbirolli had never had permanent charge of any of the big London orchestras. For this purpose, the *New York Times* had called in Ferruccio Bonavia, the well-known critic of the London *Daily Telegraph*. Bonavia, in an article headed " British estimate of Barbirolli," wrote with his usual fairness and of course from his vast knowledge of the inside of the London musical world. " The young English conductor whom New York has secured, John Barbirolli, has," he said, " made his reputation in London in spite of the faction and partisanship which are now to be found in London as well as in any other musical city. When Sir Henry Wood started his career, there was no English conductor of eminence to stand in his way. To-day there are, besides Wood, Sir Thomas Beecham, Sir Landon Ronald, Dr. Adrian Boult, Dr. Malcolm Sargent, Sir Hamilton Harty [Harty had left the Hallé in 1933], with their followers, the Beechamites, the Woodites, and the rest, whose well-grounded faith can never be shaken. Most of these are attached to concert-going organizations, so that there is not much room for guest conductors. This fact explains why Barbirolli's activities have taken him more often to the provinces than to the capital. In the great provincial centres he scored his first successes, as conductor to the now defunct British National Opera Company, on the strength of which he was invited to conduct opera at Covent Garden.

" There, too, he made his mark," Bonavia continued, " but the London public is determined never to be stampeded into an admittance of triumph where a young British artist is concerned. Its full confidence can only be won by a foreign reputation or else by long and steady wooing. In the limited time Barbirolli went as far as any man, but the provinces, or rather Scotland, gave him his finest opportunity when he was appointed to conduct the Scottish Orchestra."

Bonavia's next remark in the *New York Times* article will interest particularly readers of this book, for he said: " There is in the whole country only one other appointment carrying the same weight and the same chances—that of the Hallé Orchestra in Manchester." Bonavia had much more to say and it is worth quoting, since it fills out the picture we are presenting in this book. In Scotland, he said, " Barbirolli did so well that even London was obliged to take notice. Many years ago Sir Alexander MacKenzie spoke of Barbirolli as a modest but very exceptionally able young musician, bound to succeed. The early promise has now been fully realized. . . . Not a single orchestral performer who has played under Barbirolli has anything but praise for his tact, his skill, his ability to secure discipline without bluster.

" The effects he obtains are obviously the result of complete understanding between orchestra and conductor. He does not waste time expounding questionable philosophical tenets, but sticks to the business in hand; his requests to the players are made in that simple technical language they understand. As an ex-string player (he was, like Toscanini, an excellent 'cellist), he knows what phrasing can do for a musical work. . . . This, too, is what the hard-bitten professional understands, and rehearsals with Barbirolli have always the effect of making the men determined to do their best for him." Bonavia concludes: " Of his talent for interpreting the works of the great masters, New York musicians will soon judge for themselves. He has, however, no strong likes and dislikes. If he has special sympathies he keeps them to himself, and he will give the same care to the work of an unknown, if entrusted to him, that he does to that of a classic." No pronouncement could have done more to place Barbirolli in his right perspective. Another newspaper quoted Ernest Newman, the famous musicologist, as saying of Barbirolli that "he was one of the finest conductors Britain has ever produced ".

Side by side with such calm and considered appraisals were the big headlines announcing Barbirolli's arrival, and his preparations for his first concert at Carnegie Hall. All through that October, 1936, they trumpeted clamorously. "Youngest Maestro here," announced the *New York Evening Journal*; " English maestro will try on shoes left by Toscanini," cried the Worcester, Mass., *Herald*; " Maestro Barbirolli—He is English," piped the Greensberg, Pa., *Review*. " The Philharmonic turns a page," was the heading of an article by Lawrence Gilman, in the *New York Herald Tribune*. The headings of a two-column article by Winthrop Sargent, in the *New York American*, read: " A new hand wields the baton of the Philharmonic Symphony . . . Barbirolli's problems . . . The difficulties confronting conductor are psychological as well as technical. . . ." A *New York Daily News* headline read: " Philharmonic, 95, begins with new deal."

And while the sub-editors were busy writing headlines and the critics pontificated about him, Barbirolli, unruffled, smiling, self-assured, was answering the reporters' questions, reporters who met him at the boat, or waylaid him in the street, or stopped him on the stairs of his apartment. One interviewer wrote that on landing from the liner, Barbirolli " expressed a feeling of nervousness at filling the place occupied for so long by Toscanini. He said ' I know there are some people who feel sorry for me, but it is a wonderful opportunity for a young conductor, and I'll give the best I've got.' " To the *New York Herald Tribune* reporter he " seemed extremely modest ", and said: " I don't think

anybody could say that I am following in Toscanini's footsteps. That was one great era. It is past. Things must come
to an end. But music must go on." Barbirolli continued:
" You'll find me a very simple person—passionately fond of
music. I serve it the best way I can. I hope you'll like me.
I am looking forward to some wonderful music because I
know your orchestra is wonderful." To another interviewer
he said: " As a conductor I have to conduct music of all
schools. I am in the happy position of being catholic in my
tastes. Of course, one week I conduct the Brahms Fourth
and I think that's the best. Then next week it's Beethoven's
Seventh and that seems the best. And the third week it's
Wagner and so on. I am happy in all schools of music."

Evidently the musical dowagers of Park Avenue had heard
that Barbirolli, unlike their previous idols at Carnegie Hall,
used a score when conducting. When he was asked about
this during those first few days in New York, he did not
fumble in his reply or mince his words. He had heard that
one before. " My contention," he said, " is that, being the
privileged guardian of the work you are conducting, unless
you really know every note from memory, it is more sincere
to use a score." He was to say much on this score-or-no-
score question later, but his " it is more sincere to use a
score ", provided the New Yorkers with an early clue to
Barbirolli's quality and philosophy as a musician. Naturally
enough questions were fired at him about how he came to be
engaged, and some were a little incredulous when he told
them he did not know much more than they did about it.
One writer had observed, in speculating about the reasons,
" Possibly the New York Philharmonic directors are looking
to the future in engaging a conductor who can make an
amusing after-dinner speech, as well as direct an orchestra
and play the 'cello. But, though the Philharmonic Board
displayed commendable boldness (even if involuntary) in

putting their faith in the dark horse that is Barbirolli, ten weeks of an untried conductor may be a longer period than they would prefer." Others seemed to find an explanation in the fact that, like Toscanini, Barbirolli, besides being of Italian extraction, had a name of four syllables, ending in " i ".

To the *New York Herald Tribune* on October 28, 1936, Barbirolli himself said he had " no idea how he came to be chosen for his present high post ". He had met Arthur Judson, manager of the Philharmonic Symphony Society, once, but that had been eight years ago. Then came Judson's cable the previous April, " out of the blue ". " My first thought," Barbirolli told the newspaper, " was that it was an extraordinary thing because we in England look upon the orchestra here as being the pick of the world, but more especially did it seem extraordinary because the Maestro had been here for years and years and seemed likely to stay. It came as a complete surprise to me. In fact that side of the matter is still a mystery to me."

As the *New York Post* observed, " Barbirolli, unlike the Maestro, grants interviews." The concession was certainly useful to Barbirolli, because it enabled him to " put himself over " to the American public and to correct certain preconceptions and a few prejudices. But about the circumstances of the engagement he remained in the dark. Nor did he bother himself much about the matter. He soon had more important things to think about, and in any case it began to be obvious that a first-class reputation at home had preceded him.

He took up his domestic quarters in a big apartment building called Essex House, near Central Park, with his male secretary, and among the first things he did was to go and take a good look at Carnegie Hall. But for many days interviews with the Press occupied much of his time, often answering the same questions over and over again, asked by the representatives of different newspapers, from New York to California. To one he said, " Toscanini is unique," and, feeling his self-confidence restored, " No, I am not timid about following him." He repeated what he had said before, " I am an artist and a very simple person. I study and study and work and work and then I give all I've got." He was asked how much authority he would have in " hiring and firing" members of the orchestra, but as his appointment had not finally been confirmed he could make no answer. Eventually, of course, he was invested with the same authority as his predecessors, although he used it sparingly and with infinite tact.

About his musical plans, he told the *New York American* on October 29th—a week before his début at Carnegie Hall: " First I mean to make my programmes as interesting and attractive to the general public as possible." He promised one modern work at each event and said scores by American composers had already been submitted for his consideration. To some of these he was to give a first hearing.

Again and again the Pressmen harked back to the " how does it feel" theme. " He looked startled at the question," said the *New York Times*. " A quizzical glance and then, ' I do not intend to try and follow in Toscanini's footsteps. No one can do that. There is only one Toscanini.'" One or two of the Pressmen seemed disappointed at such modesty. They were not used to it. But he convinced all of them that he had a mind of his own and that he was in the habit of using it and intended to go on using it, even at Carnegie Hall.

Barbirolli knew only two members of the orchestra personally, the contra-bassoonist, with whom he had played in the Queen's Hall Orchestra twenty years before, and one of the 'cellists. He had not yet met the orchestra collectively.

He confessed that that would be an ordeal, and said: " The most important moment of my visit will be next Monday morning. The first orchestral rehearsal will take place then. For a conductor and an orchestra who are unknown to each other, that is the most exacting test."

He had already chosen his programme:

1. Suite for Strings *Purcell* (arranged *Barbirolli*)
2. Symphonic Poem, " The Tale the Pine Trees knew" . . . . *Arnold Bax*
3. Symphony in C major (K425) . . *Mozart*
      (Interval)
4. Symphony No. 4 in E minor . . *Brahms*

Bax's work was new to the orchestra and it was to prove a searching test of the players' reactions to their new conductor. Of the nature of this test Winthrop Sargent about this time wrote in the *New York American*;

" An orchestra is an aggregate of about a hundred beings, each with his own problems, frustrations, prejudices and preferences. And in the very emotional and personal business of making symphonic music, the human problems are likely to loom almost as large as the technical ones. The ideal conductor is not only a consummate musician, but he is the world's quickest-thinking diplomat. He has an intuitive faculty for sensing the mental, emotional and even physical states of the men under him. *He does not necessarily have to be liked by these men.* There have been great maestros who have even achieved results by inducing fear and anger. I think it was Nikisch of whom it was said that he made his men so angry that they played like angels. But the conductor does have to know how to create emotional reactions to make men play as he wishes them to, unconsciously and even in spite of themselves. The trick is done by dealing with music and emotions in their own terms."

What happened when Barbirolli met his orchestra for the first time we do not know in detail, but the players took to him at once, and their respect increased when they found he could talk to them in the language they understood. He gave them to understand that he expected them to work as hard as he did himself, but no harder, and possibly their liking for the young Englishman became firmly established when they realized he could get results without using the grim methods of some of his predecessors. At all events, the rehearsals went off to everybody's satisfaction, and the players did, in fact, " play like angels " at the first concert, on November 5, 1936, in Carnegie Hall, before an excited, curious, and expectant audience, many of whom had come prepared to scoff at this beardless young man from Holborn, London, who had ventured to step on to the podium so recently vacated by the Maestro. The rich dowagers who looked through their glasses at the figure at the desk, with baton raised, taut, grave, and confident, were still thinking of the orchestra as " Toscanini's Orchestra " when the concert began. When it ended, they were not so sure.

CHAPTER V

DÉBUT AT CARNEGIE HALL

THE scene in New York's Carnegie Hall on that night of November 5, 1936, can well be imagined. Away back in London it was "Guy Fawkes" night. Did the "young Englishman", as he stood there on the podium in the hushed silence that fell upon three thousand of New York's most cultured citizens, recall in the briefest flash of memory his own boyhood there? Did he see himself in the Holborn streets looking at the Guys made by the urchins, perhaps helping them in their annual enterprise? That old custom is based on a legend rooted in the centuries of England's parliamentary tradition. Here in New York Barbirolli was facing another and much newer tradition, the tradition of a great orchestra whose history, as was said, " was the history of music in America ".

To appreciate the significance of the moment and the atmosphere of Barbirolli's first concert, it is necessary to know something of the story of the New York Orchestra, a story not generally known here in England. For the orchestra which Barbirolli faced that night is, as has been said, the oldest (it is older than the Vienna Philharmonic by a few weeks) in the world. Its original element was the New York Philharmonic,[1] which absorbed, first the National Symphony Orchestra, and, in 1928, the New York Symphony Orchestra, which dated back to 1878. The Philharmonic

---

[1] For most of the information in this chapter I am indebted to Dorle Jarmel, of the New York Philharmonic Symphony Society.

gave its first concert on December 7, 1842. John Tyler was President of the United States, and the city of New York had fewer than 400,000 inhabitants; the war with Mexico over Texas had yet to be fought. Beethoven had been dead fifteen years, Schubert fourteen, Brahms was nine years old, Tchaikovsky two, and the first operas of Wagner and of Verdi had only recently been performed in Europe. Schumann had just finished his first symphony, and Chopin was about to enter on his summer idyll with George Sand. In England Queen Victoria was but two years a bride.

" It is perhaps significant," says Jarmel, " that Vienna, the imperial city of Haydn, Mozart, Beethoven, and Schubert, entered on its orchestral life about the same time as New York City, raw seaboard centre of an infant republic."

The idea of forming the Philharmonic came to a group of musicians one spring night in New York. They were walking down Broadway after a concert and entered a public house in Park Row known as *The Shakespeare*. " It was a famous restaurant in those days," wrote H. E. Krehbiel, in a handbook published in 1892. " It was kept by one Windust and his wife, most excellent caterers. Here the first suggestions pointing to a society like the Philharmonic were publicly made and discussed. U. C. Hill proposed the organization of a large and permanent society drawn from the best orchestral performers . . . to study and render symphonies, overtures and other classical music in such a manner as to cultivate a more general knowledge and a more correct public taste."

The first president of the new society thus formed was Ureli Corelli Hill. " There seems to be no accounting for his name," says Jarmel, " except that his father was fond of the violin. But Ureli was Yankeedom itself." He was forty at the time the orchestra was formed. Ten years earlier he had conducted the New York Sacred Music Society in the

REHEARSAL IN NEW YORK

BARBIROLLI AND ARTHUR BENJAMIN, THE COMPOSER,
BOATING NEAR WIGWAM INN, VANCOUVER, 1942

first complete performance of *The Messiah* ever given in the city. He was then a violin teacher and organizer of concerts. Later he went abroad and for two years studied under Spohr, and when he returned to New York he popularized Spohr's " School for the Violin ". And it was probably due to Hill that Spohr's works appeared so frequently on the young orchestra's programmes.

" Hill," says Jarmel, " although largely responsible for the successful launching of the Philharmonic, was himself an unfortunate man. He spent several years in the West seeking his fortune. When he came back, bankrupt, the society helped him by lending him almost all the money in the sinking-fund." He played in the orchestra until 1878 and then, seventy years old, he was retired. For a little while after that he played as an extra at Wallack's Theatre. Finally " convinced he lagged superfluous on the stage of life " he killed himself by taking morphine. In a farewell letter he wrote: " Ha, ha! The sooner I go the better."

During its first season the Philharmonic gave three concerts. There were sixty-three players in the orchestra, forty-one less than the strength of the present orchestra. For the sixteen years after the first season four concerts were given annually, increased to five during the next decade, and later to six. Now there are more than one hundred. The opening concert took place in the Apollo Rooms, on Lower Broadway, long forgotten by New Yorkers, but in its day a " popular resort for fashionable entertainments ". Krehbiel wrote: " In the concert hall chairs had not yet been introduced; the benches and pews which can still [1892] be found in some af the best-known concert rooms in England, were in use. Some of the commonest features of modern management were undreamt of. The subscribers were received at the door by several members of the orchestra, selected because of their appearance and address, who

D

escorted the subscribers to their seats. These ushers wore white gloves, paid for out of the society's exchequer, and carried long and slender rods of wood painted white as their wands of office. This custom prevailed for several years, but was finally suspended because of the opportunities for amusement it afforded for some of the younger attendants, whose animal spirits sometimes overcame their sense of decorum. In the fourth annual report it was recorded as an instance of the economical administration of the society's affairs that four dollars seventy-five cents had been saved on the sum spent for gloves over the preceding season."

Krehbiel continues: " The demeanour of the performers before coming upon the stage, as well as in the presence of the public, was most circumspect and dignified. Gathered in the ante-room with their instruments in hand, players waited until the conductor or president politely requested the oboe player to sound his instrument for the others to tune by. He would say, ' Would the oboe please give us his A? ' All the performers, except the violoncellos, played standing up."

It is recorded that the sixty-three members of this original orchestra were obliged to be " professors of music ", and it was a co-operative group, as the present London Symphony Orchestra has been for some years. The second article of the by-laws of the orchestra's constitution prohibited " all indecorum of the members . . . at all the society's meetings, viz., smoking, wearing of hats or caps, violent language, etc."

Although everybody seems to have had an education in good manners at each of the early performances, besides hearing Beethoven and Mozart symphonies played better than anywhere in America at that time, the concerts at first produced small financial results. When the orchestra was launched in 1842, " nobody in town would put up a nickel for it ". Even musicians outside the Philharmonic circle derided the whole scheme. But the members of the orchestra, besides " giving " their services, had sufficient faith in their enterprise to contribute twenty-five dollars each from their own modest means. The first season, when profits came to be divided, left each member with fifteen dollars, conductor sharing alike with violinists, trombones and French horns and the others.

The virtuoso conductor had not arrived in the world of music, and so the conductors in New York, like others everywhere, were members of the orchestra and played their instruments when not directing. A few years later the economical accounts of the orchestra contained the item: " One dollar for tin sconces; two dollars for the coach and thirteen dollars for the wine, provided by contract to the soloists, the Misses Tourney."

The orchestra had to wait more than twenty years before a permanent conductor could be engaged. On September 9, 1865, the board of directors gave the following decision in a letter to Carl Bergmann: " Resolved that Mr. Carl Bergmann be engaged as conductor to lead the concerts and necessary rehearsals of the coming season for the sum of one thousand dollars. You would confer a favour if you would acknowledge receipt of this, and state if it meets with your approbation and acceptance." The offer was accepted. There were five concerts that season, and " many of the town's musical busybodies shook their heads over the scandalously extravagant sum paid a mere conductor ". But Bergmann proved an inspired leader and during the next ten years he established " a tradition of method and interpretation which persisted long after his death ".

Bergmann was succeeded in 1879 by Theodore Thomas, in many ways a remarkable figure, whose best remembered remark is: " They don't like Wagner? Then they will have to hear him until they do! " Thomas reigned until 1891. Apart from the great work of the earlier pioneers, it was Bergmann and Thomas who shaped the musical destinies of the Philharmonic Society. Bergmann, like Thomas, had boldly espoused the cause of the " revolutionists "—Berlioz, Wagner, and Liszt. Theodore Thomas, according to one American musical historian, " did more for orchestral music in North America than any previous conductor. His name was a household word wherever a love of good music was to be found. He literally formulated and controlled musical taste the length and breadth of the land. He was the arbiter of our musical destinies. For a period he was not only the conductor of the Philharmonic Society, but ... the society itself."

The Hungarian Anton Seidl succeeded Thomas, but died suddenly in 1898. He is said to have made " venerable bones rattle " with his interpretation of Wagner and Liszt, in whose works he excelled, but he was rather negligent of the great classics which still, half a century later, form the backbone of every orchestral concert programme all over the world. The sixty-first season of the orchestra was under the direction of Walter Damrosch, after which, until 1906, there came a procession of guest conductors, all, except Victor Herbert, from abroad. So for five years or so the Society's subscribers became familiar with the personalities and methods of such outstanding European conductors and musicians as Henry Wood, Eduard Colonne, Felix Weingartner, Richard Strauss, Willem Mengelberg, and Fritz Steinbach.

The system of engaging guest conductors came to an end in 1906, and for the next three years the Russian Wassily Safonoff was at the head of the orchestra. Gustav Mahler conducted for the sixty-eighth and sixty-ninth seasons, and then, from 1911 until 1920, Josef Stransky.

It was in 1911 that Joseph Pullitzer left in his will 500,000 dollars for " perfecting the orchestra, and placing it on a more independent basis, and for increasing the number of concerts in the city at reduced rates, to give hearings to his favourite composers—Beethoven, Wagner, Liszt ". In 1921–22 the National Symphony Orchestra was merged with the Philharmonic, and for the next year Willem Mengelberg controlled the destinies of the combined orchestra. During 1924–25 Furtwangler came to New York for the first time as guest conductor, to be followed in 1925–26 by Arturo Toscanini—" a great year this ". That year and the next Toscanini shared the season with Furtwangler and Mengelberg. Then, in the spring of 1928, there was a further merger with the Philharmonic's only remaining rival—the New York Symphony Orchestra.

The New York Symphony had been founded in 1878 by Leopold Damrosch. Under his baton it took part in the first great musical festival given in New York in May 1881, at the Seventh Regiment Armory. It grew to even greater fame under Leopold's son, Walter, who took over his father's post in 1885. There were many significant milestones in its history during the next forty-three years. In the spring of 1891 Carnegie Hall was dedicated with a musical festival at which the New York Symphony played and for which Tchaikovsky came to America. The following November Paderewski gave his first New York concert with Damrosch's orchestra, and in 1897 a popular series of Symphony Concerts for Young People was inaugurated. In 1920 the orchestra went abroad under Damrosch, becoming the first American orchestra to make a foreign tour.

Ten years later the combined orchestra—now containing the cream of the players of both—toured Europe under Toscanini, with almost sensational results. Twenty-three concerts were given in fifteen different cities: London,

Paris, Zurich, Milan, Rome, Florence, Turin, Munich, Vienna, Budapest, Prague, Leipzig, Dresden, Berlin, and Brussels, and it was during its tour, in London, that Toscanini and Barbirolli first met. The 1935–36 season was Toscanini's last. He gave up a task which he " finally found too heavy ". From then on he has held the less exacting post of conductor of the N.B.C. Orchestra.

CHAPTER VI

APPOINTMENT AS MUSICAL DIRECTOR

THE concert at which Barbirolli made his début in Carnegie Hall also began the New York Philharmonic Symphony Orchestra's ninety-fifth season and Barbirolli was to be in charge for the next ten weeks. The great hall was packed to its utmost capacity. And most of those present must have felt that after all the newspapers had said of him during the past few months and all he had said to the newspapers, he was no longer a stranger except in the flesh. Many of them, as they opened their programmes, may have remembered that a few days before, Lawrence Gilman, in the *New York Herald Tribune*, had said the final word. " It is heartening to know," wrote Gilman, " that Mr. Barbirolli is an excellent programme-maker—imaginative, enterprising, experimental, wide-visioned, and catholic, yet tactful and realistic, with that instinct for audience-psychology without which even the greatest conductor must occasionally come to grief." The instinct of which Gilman here speaks had led Barbirolli from the first to realize that no work of music was complete until it had been consummated as an act of creation in the minds of an audience, and that the task of a conductor was to assist in making the consummation itself complete and lastingly satisfying. Moreover, not only was the great orchestra beginning a new season at this concert. It was felt by the public, as well as by the management, that a new chapter in its history was opening. And although other conductors were to be seen in the remaining weeks of the season, somehow it was generally assumed that the management's hopes were pinned on the " charming young gentleman from Bloomsbury ", rather than on the others. This seemed to be the significance behind the fact that Barbirolli had been chosen to open the season.

The interest of the audience must also have been quickened by the reception given to Barbirolli's programmes for those first ten weeks. Let Gilman again speak for the rest. He wrote: " They [the programmes] are among the most skilful, interesting, and provocative that have ever engaged the activities of the great orchestra which will interpret them. They include the old and the new, the well-loved, and the unknown: music that is ageless and unfading, and music that we never hear, but should. They range from Purcell to the America of to-day, from Mehul to Delius, from Schubert to Sibelius, from Mozart to Kodaly, from Bach to Franck, from Beethoven and Brahms and Wagner to Vaughan Williams and Ravel." Gilman ended: " The omens are excellent. Let us give heed to Mr. Barbirolli and welcome the Philharmonic Symphony under its new regime.

The opening programme of November 5th, a Thursday, was repeated the next afternoon and on the following Sunday afternoon in Carnegie Hall, this being the usual arrangement. During the month, both the Philadelphia and Boston orchestras also gave concerts in the hall, which was used besides by General Motors for Sunday afternoon concerts when the Philharmonic Symphony was not playing. There were recitals by Simon Barer and Mischa Elman. But the hall's chief event always was the Philharmonic Symphony Concert. On Sunday afternoon the concert was broadcast regularly over the Columbia system's network.

Of that first concert on Thursday night, Gilman reported in the New York Herald Tribune: " A short, slight, dark

young man, somewhat Napoleonic in aspect, with a hint of
Mediterranean intensity in his face, walked resolutely upon
the stage of Carnegie Hall last evening before a waiting
orchestra and audience to undertake the most formidable
task that any musical interpreter could face; that of succeeding Arturo Toscanini in New York.

" It is to be set down as one of the most noteworthy
achievements of our day that some two hours later, when
John Barbirolli brought to a close his opening programme
at the first concert of the season, he had won the respect of
the knowing ones among the audience, who had doubtless
gathered to hear him in a mood politely sceptical, waiting
to be shown."

Gilman, like the other critics, seized on the unfamiliar Bax
work, which was being given its first performance in America
(it was composed in 1933), as the single item in the programme upon which the critical faculty could have full play.
Unlike some of his colleagues, he found in it much to ponder
over. Of the performance, he wrote: " Mr. Barbirolli had
not proceeded through more than a dozen pages of the evening's novelty, before we became aware that he had mastered
that first and last secret of the fine interpreter's ability to lead
us to the heart of music; the ability to discover and to realize
the melodic impulse that gives it life and direction and
coherence. There are lovely and evocative pages in this
cryptic tone poetry of Bax; pages in which Bax the dreamer
and visionary and nature-lover, the strayed wanderer from
old, forgotten worlds of sensibility and beauty, has imposed
his visions and his memories upon a communicative orchestra—an orchestra bewitched and bewitching, murmuring to
us of magic seas and haunted, melancholy woods. Mr. Barbirolli, setting free for us the beauty of this music—especially
in the Lento expressivo section, with its cantilena sustained
and extended by the strings—reminded us that he began his

career as a player of the 'cello and a practitioner of chamber music. . . . He made the Philharmonic's sumptuous and enamouring strings sound at times like musing and retrospective lovers, like bardic rhapsodists and poets."

Gilman ended his notice thus: " For Mr. Barbirolli, to judge from his achievements last evening, is something better and rarer and finer than a conductor of power and sensibility. He permits us to think that he is akin to those uncommon interpreters who give us a measure of ' that inner standard of distinction, selection and refusal ' which an incorruptible artist once defined. . . ."

This notice occupied a column of space in the *New York Herald Tribune*. In the *New York Times*, Olin Downes was less lyrical and more critical than his colleague Gilman. " Mr. Barbirolli makes his orchestra *sound* . . . His predilection is for a full-blooded tone, and his excitement was felt by the audience. Also evident was a tension and lack of composure very understandable in the circumstances," he said.

Downes calls Bax's *The Tale the Pine Trees Knew* a "very poor piece of music . . . nebulous and imitative, possessed of most of the vices of the semi-impressionistic Celtic school and none of the distinguished qualities of Bax's best scores. It is far from the power and fine, rugged lines of the last two Bax symphonies. The piece served to show the conductor as interpreter of music of a certain type, but it cannot be said that it ranks as an addition to the Philharmonic Symphony repertory." After making the curious statement that " the season is young to play a Mozart symphony . . . with the classic style it requires ", Downes goes on: " For me the best part of the evening was offered by the last two movements of the Fourth Brahms symphony, where there was exceptional virility, grip and lyrical opulence, and on occasion, the impact of the bear's paw. The *tempo* of the

first part of the *scherzo* was the right one—a *tempo* of rugged
Brahms individualism. Perhaps the *trio* was rather slow, a
little sentimental. In general this was a red-blooded, dramatic and grandly constructed reading.

" Of earlier passages not so much could be said. These
movements were somewhat episodic, having in places one
tempo and the true accent, in other places missing the
essence of the composer's thinking. But the variations of
the celebrated *passacaglia* were read with a fine versatility
of expression, now in a poetic, now in a heroic spirit.
At the end, the audience gave Mr. Barbirolli resounding
applause."

About Barbirolli himself, Downes wrote: " Mr. Barbirolli's manner on the platform is ingratiating and uninten-
tionally demonstrative as the musical afflatus seizes him. It is
a pleasure to record that he conducts from score, and not
from memory, in the ridiculous and unnecessary way in
which certain celebrated conductors find it necessary to
imitate Toscanini. It was evident that, in more than one
instance, Mr. Barbirolli could have led without score, had
it been necessary. He did not choose thus to exhibit himself
and thus make matters more risky and less certain for the
players of the orchestra." For the rest, Downes says " it will
be time to estimate him in detail as an interpretive musician
after we have heard him in half-a-dozen concerts. But his
American début gained him a very favourable reception."

In the *World Telegram*, Pitts Sanborn wrote: "The
familiar Brahms symphony was done with abounding energy,
with some unusual ideas as to pace and a prevailing tem-
pestuousness that had hardly been emphasized here so
strongly in previous performances . . . Mr. Barbirolli, small,
trim and dynamic, was cordially received by the large
audience. He proved to be as active a batonist as has
occupied the Philharmonic Symphony podium, even if some

of his activity may be attributed to the nervousness of a trying
début. . . . The audience applauded vigorously at the end
of each number. Thus began the new season of the Philharmonic Symphony Society."

W. J. Henderson, in the *New York Sun*, said of Bax's
work: " What these pines knew was how to sigh and moan
and urge Mr. Bax to deeds of instrumentation. There was
good stuff in the symphonic poem, but it was not concisely
nor directly conveyed to the audience . . . It was so strung out
that one was grateful that Mr. Bax had seen only Norwegian
pines and Scotch firs and had not got into the redwood
district of California." Of the conductor, Henderson said:
" It was surely a trying night for him and over-anxiety may
have accounted for some overstressing of points, some
heavily marked *sforzandi*, and some almost rude contrasts.
But this is a young musician who has a good sense of the
orchestra, backed by sound training and valuable experience.
That he is a master of his craft could not be determined by
last evening's concert. . . . For those who enjoy orchestral
concerts by watching the conductor, Mr. Barbirolli will be
welcome. He is very active and puts a power of physical
labour into his job. Those who prefer to concentrate on the
technics of conducting will find that this young man is well
acquainted with them. He has a very vigorous beat and
when he gives his men their entrance cues he employs a
sign language well suited to reminding them of his rehearsal
instructions and keeps a close watch on their *tempi* and
dynamics."

In contrast, there was this from another critic: " Mr.
Barbirolli came to us unknown, meagre of reputation,
unheralded, a wholly unsensational apparition. He has disclosed himself as a musician of taste and fire and intensity,
electric, vital, sensitive, dynamic, experienced . . . He has
mastered not only his temperament but his trade. He is

already at thirty-six a conductor of impressive authority, delicacy and imagination."

Oscar Thompson, in *Musical America* of November 10th, wrote: " If Barbirolli was nervous, the signs of it were not to be noted in his demeanour. He came briskly to the platform and went briskly about the business of making music. A listener, who was late in reaching his seat in the middle of one of the front rows after the interval, found himself the object of a podium stare that continued until its object had settled in his chair. . . . Though Barbirolli sometimes glanced at the scores that were open before him, and turned their pages, it was evident that he could have presented this entire concert from memory, if this had been his desire."

There remains one other opinion that should be quoted. Winthrop Sargent wrote in the *New York American*: " From the first note . . . it was obvious that the new conductor possessed the fundamental gifts of leadership and temperament. He is able to convey musical ideas directly and dynamically by means of gesture. He is able to sustain and alter his *tempi* with accuracy and conviction. He knows how to build up his climaxes and how to balance the ingredients of a symphonic work with poise and restraint. . . . It was in Mozart's C major Symphony that Mr. Barbirolli met his first big test of the evening. . . . The test as a whole was well met. It was a scholarly and poised interpretation that the conductor offered his audience. The *finale* in particular disclosed a brilliancy and finish that make one look forward with pleasure and anticipation to his future appearance." Winthrop Sargent, in the course of this notice, also refers to the " always somewhat conservative Thursday night audience ".

This criticism reveals a sincere effort to give the new conductor a fair hearing and to refrain from making obvious—

and useless—comparisons. But the impression which it chiefly conveys was that Barbirolli had acquitted himself much better than some people had expected. His performance, not to put it too strongly, evidently came as a revelation to those among the critics and the audience who had been inclined to despair of ever again hearing music played as the orchestra had played it under Toscanini. Barbirolli had " shown them ".

Almost every newspaper in the country, through its New York correspondent, reported the concert at considerable length, and all of them agreed that a new musical force had arrived from Britain of whom they would have to take note. Fortunately, perhaps, it is not the music critics who determine the pattern of a conductor's future. Although in the years to come Barbirolli, like every previous conductor of the orchestra, not excluding Toscanini, was to be the object of adverse criticism, much of it ill-considered and irresponsible, as long as he retained the confidence of the orchestra, the management and the public that filled Carnegie Hall at his concerts, he was content. A few days after his début, while discussion still raged, the New York correspondent of the *Christian Science Monitor*, one of the world's greatest newspapers, published in Boston, wrote: " This young conductor was very sure of himself, and of his job. It was evident that he had the indispensable quality of authority. He was not feeling his way. He knew perfectly where he was going, and he was doing the leading. This is a hopeful sign. An orchestra like the Philharmonic Symphony does not yield allegiance to everybody who waves a stick over it."

For his first Sunday concert, Barbirolli substituted the Elgar *Enigma Variation* for the Mozart symphony, and the change seems to have been a success. Then came the second Thursday evening concert at Carnegie Hall, with the same " somewhat conservative " audience, to hear a mainly Beethoven programme. The symphony was the Second, in D major, and Marjorie Lawrence was the soloist in an aria from *Fidelio*. The programme ended with excerpts from Wagner's *Gotterdammerung*.

This second concert gave the critics the chance either to revise or confirm their impressions. Olin Downes, in the *New York Times*, wrote: " John Barbirolli gave his second Thursday night concert, and with marked success. It is a pleasure to say that he was more in his element than on the trying occasion of his first performance." Downes is not so didactic as he was about Barbirolli's *tempi* and about other details of the performances. There are many favourable " perhapses ".

"The orchestra played the *Fidelio* overture superbly ", Downes went on. " The composition was given a virtuoso performance, and by so much we notice that Mr. Barbirolli is a conductor of whom much pleasure may be anticipated. . . ." Of Wagner's music: " Barbirolli flung himself into it, revelled in it and exulted in drawing from the band the fullest measure of its sonorities."

Lawrence Gilman, in the *New York Herald Tribune*, con-fined himself to the Wagner music, saying finally: " This newly-recovered Wagner is in the great tradition—unhurried, unminimized, uncompressed; large in span and implication, uttering that noble and exalted beauty without which Wagner does not live."

W. J. Henderson, in the *Sun*, mentions that the *Gotterdammerung* sequence had been arranged by Barbirolli himself, with " liaisons uniting the separate units ", and " bridges made up of materials drawn from the *Nibelung* dramas, not from the conductor's fancy ".

After the first two weeks' concerts it had become clear to everybody that Barbirolli had made his mark. Indeed, this became so evident that the management did not wait much

longer to announce his appointment as musical director and
regular conductor for the whole of the three following
seasons. The announcement was made public in the Press
at the beginning of December. Thus Barbirolli became the
first full-time permanent conductor of the orchestra since
Josef Stransky occupied the post in 1921, for Toscanini,
although conductor-in-chief, had not been tied down by a
contract during the previous ten years.

The Board of Directors of the Philharmonic Symphony
Orchestra, in their official statement, said: "The appointment [of Mr. Barbirolli] marks a new era in the history of
the society. It is the solution, the board feels, of several
major issues which have confronted the Philharmonic for
some time: the need of a young conductor of artistic
integrity who could build towards the orchestra's future as
well as enhance its present; for a director whose talents are
recognized in such specific terms as increased audiences; for
a man strong and vital enough to mould the orchestra into
a consistent personality and technical unity. In Mr. Barbirolli the society believes this threefold problem can be
solved."

The statement then refers to the improvement in attendance at the Philharmonic concerts under Barbirolli, and goes
on: "A proportion of the augmented ticket sale could be
accounted for by the general improvement in business conditions, but a large part of it is obviously due to the hold Mr.
Barbirolli has gained on the music-lovers of this city in the
eighteen concerts he has conducted here since his début
programme on November 5th." This decision actually came
after only three weeks had gone of the ten weeks alloted to
Barbirolli.

Soon he was being made the guest of honour at many
public social functions. On November 13th it was announced that a tea would be given in his honour by the

STUDIES IN EXPRESSION

Smith College Club and the newspapers published a list of about a hundred names of influential people who would attend. But most of the time left over from concerts he gave to rehearsals and to private study in his bachelor quarters in Essex House. He had become in America a celebrity in his own right almost overnight, just as this had happened not ten years since in London.

Before the season in New York was over, he returned to Glasgow to finish the 1936–37 season there with the Scottish Orchestra, whose management had decided to release him from his engagement, feeling, as has been said, that their conductor's new appointment and the resounding successes at Carnegie Hall which had brought it about, were things that honoured them, as well as him. The New York Orchestra's season did not last all the year round as in the case with leading British orchestras nowadays, so that in any case there was a long vacation for the conductor and orchestra, during which the conductor at least was free to accept engagements in other parts of the United States. Over the course of the next three years Barbirolli enlarged his experience in this way. His services were in great demand because of his prestige as permanent conductor of the New York Orchestra. The 1937–38 season in New York was one of continued triumph for Barbirolli, and by the time the next season came in sight, " Munich " had happened.

CHAPTER VII

A BRILLIANT SEASON

THE 1938–39 season of the New York Philharmonic Symphony was one of particular brilliance. Among the soloists engaged were Sergei Rachmaninoff, Artur Schnabel, Jascha Heifetz, Kirsten Flagstad, Artur Rubinstein, Mischa Elman, Walter Gieseking, José Iturbi, and Adolph Busch.

The *New Yorker*, on October 22, 1938, continued this note under a sketch of Barbirolli: " Now beginning his third season with the New York Philharmonic, and still, at thirty-eight, the youngest conductor in the country. His friends call him Tita. He smokes forty English cigarettes a day, freely indulges his fondness for York ham and fine wines, and is something of an authority on the history of medicine. His instrument is the 'cello." About the same date the London *Evening News* contained a Reuter report from New York which said : " Mr. John Barbirolli, the popular London conductor, was last night given an ovation at the opening of the 1938–39 season of the New York Philharmonic Symphony Orchestra under his direction at Carnegie Hall (New York's Queen's Hall). Afterwards well-wishers crowded the dressing-room, congratulating and welcoming Barbirolli." The season was to last twenty-eight weeks, and Barbirolli was in charge for twenty-six of the twenty-eight. An advertisement in the *New York Times* announced that all the balcony seats at fourteen dollars were sold out.

The main work at the opening concert was Beethoven's Fifth Symphony, which had been played at the society's first

concert ninety-six years before. War loomed threateningly
in the air in that October of 1938. The day before the opening concert the Philharmonic Symphony League held its
usual luncheon, and Mr. Sokolovsky rose to say: "America's
unique responsibility in the world of our time, which we
have to accept whether we like it or not, is that of preserving
the fruits of Western Civilization. There may soon be no
other place in the world where music can be heard without
the intervention of politics. . . . We have got to do in the
twentieth century what Germany did for human culture in
the nineteenth century, and we have got to prepare ourselves
for it." This speaker could not, of course, foresee how music
was to flourish in Britain even at the height of peril, but he
gave an edge to what many Americans, with their limited
horizon, were thinking.

So the Philharmonic Symphony season started off with a
flourish. Before it ended Hitler had marched into Czechoslovakia and was threatening Poland. In the midst of all the
alarm and despair, Barbirolli and his men provided ever more
glittering distractions in Carnegie Hall. And Ben Gross
provided a small diversion of his own for his readers in the
New York Daily News. "Beethoven's Fifth Symphony
which Barbirolli led yesterday," he wrote, "was also presented [on the air with the N.B.C. Orchestra] by Toscanini
on Saturday night. So I had five musically untrained persons
tune into both concerts. Four of them found no difference
whatever in the two performances. The fifth one did. Here's
his report: 'Barbirolli's orchestra seemed to have a richer
volume. But Toscanini's, at times, was more dramatic and
played with a much more lilting and singing effect.'"

Leading critics had evidently left Carnegie Hall for their
offices before the second half of the programme, so did not
hear Barbirolli's rendering of the Fifth Symphony on the
opening night. But Olin Downes, in the New York Times,

in the course of a column-long notice, wrote of Barbirolli:
" It is a pleasure to chronicle that his performance (of the
Freischutz overture) so youthful and gallant in spirit, was
distinguished by taste, as well as his native enthusiasm."

The Houston (Texas) Post's correspondent, Herbert
Roussel, made a big feature of the comparison between Barbirolli and Toscanini afforded by the Fifth Symphony. The
headlines of his article ran: " Barbirolli gets decision over
Toscanini in tilt of musical heavyweights." " Collision of
two maestri with Beethoven's Fifth appears to leave Britan-
nia ruling the waves."

Roussel's article had value chiefly because it represented
the feelings of many people in America interested less in
symphonic music than in the personalities of its interpreters.
" Anybody who listened to the two performances of Beethoven's Fifth Symphony on Saturday night [Toscanini's],
and Sunday afternoon [Barbirolli's]," he wrote, " must have
realized that unusual business was going on. The long
threatened direct comparison between Arturo Toscanini and
John Barbirolli, the man who replaced him as head of the
New York Philharmonic, was being offered to light up the
beginning of another season of aerial music. It may have
been purely accidental "—it was—" that Toscanini and
Barbirolli should have carded the same piece to be played at
a couple of concerts given within twenty-four hours, but it
seems a strange bit of coincidence. Barbirolli, of course, was
the heretic. When Mr. Toscanini interprets one of the
classics, it is supposed to stay fully and finally interpreted
for that week, at least, and it is rare and presumptuous for any
other conductor having use of the same air to come along
with his own remarks on the subject the following day."

Then, under a sub-heading, " Testing the Superman
Theory ", Roussel continues: " The Englishman is doubtless a realist. It is hardly likely that he is among those who

68

believe all that is written and spoken about the glory and
celestial rightness of every tempo and intonation of the great
Italian. . . . Mr. Barbirolli . . . probably feels he has a
better orchestra than Toscanini has been able to make of
the N.B.C. organization as yet, and he thought the moment
was right for a showdown."

Anyone who knows Barbirolli will realize that anything
like a " showdown with Toscanini " would have been the
thing farthest from his thoughts.

But let Roussel proceed: " In my judgement," he wrote,
" it turned out that it was. But even if he had not a motive
of that kind, Barbirolli could hardly have known with what
sweetness his plan would materialize. Samuel Chotzinoff,
N.B.C.'s symphony commentator, during the intermission
of Toscanini's performance . . . in ten minutes of unbroken
obeisance, with occasional help from Lawrence Gilman, proceeded to restate the canonical basis of the Toscanini religion
and make it clear to the listener that in music there is no
god but the Big Boy and that he alone brings us the true
message and meaning of Beethoven."

Roussel next deals with the two performances, first with
that of Toscanini's, and then with Barbirolli's. " Mr. Toscanini," he wrote, " then offered the Fifth. It was a strange
and individual reading, beginning with an almost staccato
sounding of the ' fate ' notes and continuing on lickety-split
through the first movement, with a sort of delicate briskness
suggestive of Mozartian measures. The climaxes were taken
with a noble and superhuman restraint. The famed brio
was held to a minimum. Always there was a whipping-up of
the tempo . . . In the end, Mr. Toscanini's achievement, in
my case at least, was to make the Fifth sound for the first
time like a nervous man telling his troubles, rather than a
Titan shaking a violent fist at fate. I do not question the
beautiful development of every movement, but I do say that

Mr. Toscanini gave to it an effect that aroused no emotion in my breast.

" Sunday afternoon Barbirolli came along to read the Fifth in exactly the opposite manner. Where Toscanini had pinched in for meticulous nuance, subordinating smashing effects to his desire for illuminating underlying material, the English conductor went for the big thrills. He let out the Philharmonic as it has seldom been let out before. He made Beethoven rage and jubilate with the voice of thunder, and he hung on to the ' fate ' notes till his horn players were blue in the face.

" In this treatment the whole piece becomes a leaping and brilliant flame of defiances. The orchestra took fire from the first and has never played with more dramatic effect in any programme I have had the luck to enjoy. You were shaken when that music was over. . . . It seemed to me that Beethoven entered Carnegie Hall to announce that he had been misquoted the night before. Mr. Barbirolli was lucky to be present as master of ceremonies. The English badly needed a victory of some kind." There was a sting in that last phrase for most Englishmen—" The English badly needed a victory of some kind."

During the summer of 1938 Barbirolli had been in England. " Three weeks ago," wrote William G. King, in the New York Sun, on Barbirolli's return to New York in October, " he'd have bet you his last baton that he'd never again hurry across that space between the wings and the podium of Carnegie Hall, rap sharply on his score rack, and feel the glory of music rising under his hands. He thought he'd be in the trenches—' just an animal, you know, eating, sleeping, and fighting, and not thinking or feeling beyond those things.' For John Barbirolli, veteran of the last World War, is still a reserve officer in the British Army and if war had come over Czechoslovakia, he'd have been among the first to go. Such a war, he thinks, would have ended everything for him, even if he'd survived it."

Barbirolli himself said at that time: " I'm on my third career now. Solo 'cellist, quartet leader, conductor. I think a fellow can pick up the pieces just so often—and this time, I doubt there'd have been many pieces left for anybody." He explained that he had been in London that night a month before when Chamberlain said it looked as if war had been inevitable. " I wonder," he said, " if you can realize how close it all seemed over there. The little, horribly significant things, were what brought it home to you. I saw my sister trying a gas mask on my baby niece. Do you know, the postal authorities actually distributed postal cards with tickets of evacuation from London, so refugees could notify their relatives where they had been taken? I like to think that's a typically English touch."

That summer he had spent hard at work in England— completing the suite from the entr'acte music of Debussy's *Pelleas and Melisande*, and pouring over manuscript scores in the British Museum and elsewhere, for, as was said by another New York musical columnist, " he is a firm believer in cutting back through traditional interpretations to get at the music as the composer himself set it down ".

During the same summer months in England he was also busy arranging his programmes for the forthcoming season at Carnegie Hall.

He settled to his own satisfaction a controversy about the Mozart *Adagio and Fugue* for strings (K546) which was to figure in the opening programme of the series. This work had been originally composed for two pianos. Later Mozart arranged it for strings and Koechel published it as the 27th String Quartet. Barbirolli's friend Andre Mangeot had found the original manuscript of the *Fugue* in the British Museum, and it proved beyond doubt that Mozart had intended the work for string orchestra. "The *Fugue* is a version made by Mozart himself from the *Fugue* for two pianos, composed on December 29 1783," Barbirolli said. "He made his arrangement for strings on June 26, 1788, completing it with an *Adagio* introduction. These two pieces were published by Koechel with the sub-title '27th Quartet'. The whereabouts of the manuscript of the *Adagio* is at present unknown, but it is obvious from the manuscript of the *Fugue* that Mozart intended it for string orchestra, for I found he wrote separate lines for the 'cello and basses with, of course, different parts, his two staves being clearly marked in his own handwriting 'violoncelli' and 'contrabassi'. Apart from this evidence, the whole piece sounds as unsatisfactory for string quartet as it is magnificent for orchestra."

Barbirolli and Arturo Toscanini crossed to New York in the same liner, the *Normandie*, and spent much of the voyage together. The *New York Sun* reported that "they both got a laugh from the sensation-seeking London paper which telephoned Barbirolli in mid-ocean to ask if it were 'likely that both you and Mr. Toscanini will conduct at the ship's concert'." Barbirolli said that on this trip Toscanini told him—they were talking of autographs, which Toscanini refused to sign—that he had only one signed photograph of a celebrity. "Toscanini got it early in his career," relates Barbirolli. "Once, after he had conducted *Falstaff*, the critics rated him unmercifully. Verdi was still alive and he had read the reviews. He called Boito, who had heard the performance, and asked him if it had been as terrible as the critics said. Boito said that, on the contrary, it was excellent. So Verdi, the very day the notices had appeared, autographed his photograph and sent it to Toscanini." Toscanini again recalled on that occasion how he had played the 'cello in the Brescia orchestra as a lad of seventeen, when Barbirolli's grandfather was the leader of the orchestra (called " concert master " by the Americans).

Of Barbirolli's arrival back in New York, one newspaper said: " John Barbirolli could have held an informal rehearsal of the Philharmonic Symphony on the *Normandie's* pier yesterday afternoon, if the boys had thought to bring their instruments along. Piastro [leader of the orchestra], Schuster, Corigliano, Varni, and Van Praag, were a few of those who came to welcome the young conductor. The *Normandie* also brought Arturo Toscanini, but Maestro did no pausing on the pier. He was spirited away as soon as the ship docked, leaving his baggage to be seen through the Customs by friends. No hits, no runs, and no errors in his encounter with the Press on this arrival."

Barbirolli had by that time made his home in an apartment block called Hampshire House.

Among the novelties and revivals planned by Barbirolli for the 1938–39 season at Carnegie Hall were Boccherini's *Sinfonia* in A, Debussy's *Berceuse Héroïque*, Arnold Bax's Fourth Symphony, Stravinsky's *Rossignol*, Prokofiev's Second Viola Concerto, Berlioz's *Les Francs-Juges* Overture, Anis Fuleihan's Piano Concerto, and compositions that had won contests for American composers. There were evenings devoted to the works of Rachmaninoff, with the composer as soloist. For Easter Sunday there was Rossini's *Messe Solemnelle*.

As the season proceeded, observers noted that in the " standard classics " the orchestra, under Barbirolli, often rose to new heights and continued to " play like angels " during the whole of this, the conductor's third season in New York. His programmes were broad enough for any man, and it is doubtful whether, at that time, any concert programmes being performed in London could compare with them for adventurousness. And all this showed that Barbirolli had won the complete confidence of the Carnegie Hall public, so much so that they would take anything he chose to give them. They had come to feel that the introduction of an unfamiliar work into the programme signified that Barbirolli had a new experience to communicate to them. And they were seldom disappointed.

It is possible that the brilliance of this last pre-war season has never been surpassed. Barbirolli was working with an enormous zest. He had completely established his authority with the orchestra, and since it was composed of many men of different European strains, he had the additional advantage in his dealings with them of being, besides an Englishman, a true cosmopolitan. This, too, suited the polyglot population of New York.

Early in the season he was telling the members of the Philharmonic Symphony League: "No *tempo* should be so slow as to make it difficult for a melody to be recognizable, and no *tempo* so fast as to make a melody unrecognizable, and a composer's metronome marks, though sometimes inaccurate, are, at any rate, a guide dangerous to ignore." Then he revealed to them that: "I have sometimes spent weeks reading scores of which 90 per cent must finally be rejected, not because they were all unworthy of performance, but because I have never believed, nor will I ever believe, that the Philharmonic Symphony concerts should become an experimental forum."

Of one of the early programmes, Olin Downes wrote in the *New York Times*: "Mr. Barbirolli dared to be very broad in his *tempi* and thus permitted the orchestra to sing the Brahms melodies in a full-throated manner." Apart from his music New York was getting to know Barbirolli himself better. He was one of the most discussed young men in town. His birthday fell on the same day as that of Gus Wade, aged eighty-three, doorman of Carnegie Hall at the

Fifty-sixth Street entrance. Wade had been doorman for
forty-six years. So they made a birthday cake for them both,
with thirty-nine candles for Barbirolli, and eighty-three for
Gus Wade—112 lighted candles in all. Wade, who had
been a flautist with the Grenadier Guards before going to
America, had known personally all the famous conductors
of the orchestra during his day—they had to pass through
his door. "They are not hard to get along with," Wade
would say. "Temperament or no temperament, if you treat
them nice they will treat you nice," an opinion quoted
beneath a picture showing Barbirolli and Gus Wade shaking
hands over their joint birthday cake.

"After the concert," it was reported, "Mr. Barbirolli
entertained his musicians with a party at the Hotel Astor, to
which Mr. Wade was invited. At midnight the men presented him with a watch and chain."

This pen portrait, written by Abram Chasins, appeared in
Vogue: "The odd part about Barbirolli is that the subscribers see the same Barbirolli that the orchestra sees—
except for his clothes. For rehearsals he exchanges the
sharply fitting evening clothes for a black Russian blouse,
buttoned to the neck, and wears over it a little military jacket.
When he talks, he spreads his feet wide apart, rocks on his
heels, and thrusts his hands deep into his trouser pockets,
like a boy showing off his first pair of long pants. He punctu-
ates his sentences by tossing back his hair with the finality of
an exclamation-point. Rehearsals have an air of quiet hard
work, with little fear of explosion. In the half-hour before
rehearsals begin, Barbirolli disposes of all the details. As his
boys drift in he asks about their families, for the orchestra
as an intricate organization weighs on him.

"There is almost always fun those few moments before
the baton raps and the rehearsal is on. Sometimes, it is just
a remark by Signor Labate, the superb oboist of the orchestra,

75

who is so small that, when he rises to address the conductor, the men shout at him, ' stand up, stand up '. The other morning when two works had been scheduled, one a Schubert symphony requiring the oboe, and the other a Mozart, which did not, Labate waddled up to Barbirolli, ' Ey, Maestro, good morn. What we play, Motz? ' To that Barbirolli replied, ' No, Schub '. Before the rehearsal ever starts Barbirolli has spent hours getting ready for it. In his apartment, twenty-eight stories high on Central Park South, he prepares scores until three and four in the morning—phrasing, fingering, correcting, bowing and re-bowing the parts.... A strict disciplinarian, Barbirolli has won the hearts of the orchestra by his musicianship . . . Handling each problem with firmness and diplomacy, without histrionics and bullying, he pulls the orchestra along. But rehearsals just the same are tense, overcast with a faint haze of fear.

" Unlike most conductors Barbirolli accepts few invitations in the season. Instead he works on scores until early in the morning, relaxing by leaving his work table, which is a mass of scissors, paste, scores, parts, pencils, knives, erasers, to go downstairs to an all-night drug store. There he sits on a stool drinking coffee. In New York he lives alone; in London with his mother. Curious, probing, enthusiastic, he loves to tell stories, which he acts, moving his arms, using his fingers as though each were an actor—wonderful stories about how he took over the conducting of a company at Covent Garden at such short notice (Beecham being indisposed) that he had only five hours' rehearsal in all for four Italian operas; about opera singers who fake the words and notes of Wagner; about the magnificent Labate, who is a story-teller's dream-child.

" In his small kitchen, Barbirolli cooks for his friends his own version of ' Spaghetti Milanese '. He does not eat, of course, before performances. But one night last winter after a concert, which had gone extremely well, he unexpectedly accepted a last-minute invitation. Unprepared to go out, he arrived in a soft tan shirt and his beautifully tailored tails. He carried off the costume with poise, but, when he found that he would be the thirteenth at table, he charmingly, but firmly, backed away. Friends who have luncheon appointments with him rarely meet him at his apartment; the hazards of getting any luncheon at all are too great. He seats them on the piano bench, facing a four-hand version of some orchestral piece. While Barbirolli plays, he bellows the second trombone voice, or any other missing voice. That is Barbirolli now [January 1939]. Right now he is at a satisfying point, the middle point in his career. When Toscanini was thirty-eight he was conducting in the pit at the Metropolitan Opera House. When Koussevitzky was thirty-eight, he was the best-known conductor in Russia. When Stokowski was thirty-eight he was just taking over the Philadelphia Orchestra. And Barbirolli at thirty-eight, is the Master of the Philharmonic Symphony Orchestra of New York."

CHAPTER VIII

PLANS FOR AN EXTENSIVE TOUR

THE portrait of Barbirolli which ended the last chapter presented him as he was about the middle of January 1939. A few days later he was giving his views on the size of the orchestra needed for Mozart to the *New York Sun*. He referred to the " ever recurring and disturbing problem of the size of the orchestra to be used in modern auditoriums when performing a Mozart symphony ", and goes on to say :

" Quite obviously some of these symphonies, which have only two oboes and two horns in addition to the strings, can only be performed with any sense of balance if the modern complement of strings is reduced. But some of the bigger works, like the *Jupiter*, the so-called *Linz*, and the great E flat, present different problems. I have experimented at rehearsals with different combinations and have come to the conclusion that for the bigger works perhaps the most satisfactory solution is to employ all the violins, about eight violas instead of twelve, six 'cellos, and four to six double-basses (since these parts are mostly a mere doubling). I was delighted, when reading some Mozart letters this summer, to find that these proportions were almost those used by Mozart himself.

" I think it proves that in certain of the bigger works, at any rate, Mozart thought of and demanded, not an emasculated preciosity, but all the virility and beauty that an extended string section can give."

Barbirolli was also asked to give his opinion on the question of applause between movements of a symphony. " Personally," he said, " I prefer to have the public save their applause for the end, because the mood and organic structure of a symphony usually profit by sustained and unbroken attention. However, in the case of a few symphonies, I think that applause between movements is only the normal reaction of any sensitive audience. This is likely to happen, for instance, after the third movement of the Tchaikovsky *Pathetique*, or the *pizzicato* movement of the Tchaikovsky Fourth. In fact, the third movement of the *Pathetique* often gets a greater public response than the end, which concludes on a soft, tragic note. Occasionally I am surprised. The other day, for instance, after the slow movement of the *Haydn* symphony in D major, the audience burst into instinctive and unexpected applause. I personally never acknowledge applause between the movements of a symphony, but I understand it when it happens. I do not encourage it, but I do not object when it occurs. The audience-reaction is often unpredictable. It is probably these uncertain elements in any audience which have given rise to the prevalent compromise—that of waiting until the end of a work before applauding."

It was by contributing to such discussions in the Press that Barbirolli made his personality and the workings of his mind more accessible to the thousands who enjoyed his concerts, either in Carnegie Hall or over the Columbia radio network. He became more alive, more real, less of a baton-wielding enigma. He impressed the New Yorkers because he not only had his own way of doing things but was also always ready to give his reasons. To that extent he made his performances more interesting and wove himself more intimately into the pattern of the city's musical life. He was always giving the critics and musical public talking points,

which in turn led to debates that enlarged their knowledge
and their musical experiences.

While Barbirolli was expounding his thoughts on the
size of Mozart's orchestra and the aesthetics of applause,
his performance of Elgar's Second Symphony in Carnegie
Hall had caused Olin Downes to write things in the New
York Times which evoked indignant comment among that
newspaper's readers. Downes had written of the work that
it was " a lengthy, pompous, bourgeois sort of thing; that it
reflects the complacency and stodginess of the era of the
antimacassar and pork-pie bonnets; that it is affected by the
poor taste and the swollen orchestral manner of the post-
romantics, without the saving graces which make the
extravagances and excrescences of a composer like Richard
Strauss acceptable ". Downes need scarcely have added, " It
happens that I do not admire this symphony. I never have."
All of which in reply to one reader who wrote: " You are
evidently striving earnestly to merit a bronze plaque for an
anti-Elgar Society. What else could conceivably account for
for the fantastic viciousness of your attack last week upon
this second symphony, which has already suffered enough
from neglect. . . . incidentally, poor Mr. Barbirolli must have
felt flattered indeed by your finding him so ' exceptionally
at home ' in this poisonous atmosphere of pork-pie bonnets
and antimaccassars." Downes ends the argument with:
" As for Mr. Barbirolli's feelings on the subject, if he read
the article at all, we feel certain he remained unmoved. He
should, and does, choose his symphonies as independently
of Press reactions as we endeavour to write regardless of his
estimates of symphonies—and fair enough." Of the same
performance of Elgar's Second, Oscar Thompson wrote in
the New York Sun: " Mr. Barbirolli devoted nearly an hour
to a lusty exposition of Elgar's Second Symphony, which
never has been and possibly never will be, overplayed on

this side of the Atlantic. His reward was applause of the type known as friendly. The work is over-long for its material, a criticism that applies about equally to each of the four movements. . . . There is honest oak in this symphony. It has breadth and it has intensity. The scoring is rich. The work moves and everything sounds. But there is about it something of the ponderosity of the Edwardian age it celebrates. . . ." That, and the " applause of the type known as friendly " was the highest praise New York had for Elgar's Second.

As Christmas approached, Barbirolli found plenty of engagements outside his regular music to distract him. The Philharmonic Symphony had been engaged as the principal orchestra to play at the New York World's Fair, which was to open the following April, and he was busy on the programmes for the series of concerts to be given. There was, too, the annual Christmas Party for the orchestra members' children, of which Barbirolli was the donor, with Edmund Roelofsina, the bass clarinet, as Santa Claus. This was held on December 20th, in the Carnegie Chamber Music Hall, after a rehearsal of the orchestra. Musical America reported: " Yoicha Hiraoki, xylophonist, and the Philharmonic Symphony Quartet provided a musical introduction to the festivities, after which sleigh bells announced the arrival of Santa Claus. Entertainment was provided by Craig Earl, ' Professor Quiz ' of the radio, and by acrobats and jugglers from Hamid's Circus of the World's Fair. After these performances, Mr. Barbirolli led the distribution of gifts and cut the cake. The children ranged in age from two to thirteen and a half years."

For Christmas Barbirolli gave the Carnegie Hall patrons a programme of Yuletide music (with Beethoven's Fourth Symphony " for those who are not Christmas-minded "), and the work which created the deepest impression was Vaughan

F 81

Williams's *Fantasia* on *Christmas Carols*, for orchestra, male chorus, and baritone solo; a " remarkable work," said Olin Downes, " that mingles grave and gay songs of Wassail and narratives of the fall of man in one delightful confusion."

A few months later, Barbirolli came out in public as a 'cellist, " for the first time in America ". The occasion was the Twelfth Night Celebration at the New York Lotus Club. Others on the programme were the Vienna Boys' Choir, and Lucig Monroe, lyric soprano. The musical items were followed by a pageant in costume, a wassail bowl procession and other traditional ceremonies. Barbirolli played quartet selections with Mishel Piastro, leader (or " concert master ") of the New York Philharmonic Symphony Orchestra, and John Corigliano, violinists and William Primrose, viola. A few nights later, at Carnegie Hall, Barbirolli's programme included the Second Brahms Piano Concerto, with Artur Schnabel at the piano. A week later he had Artur Rubinstein as soloist in the Mozart A major Concerto. On April 30th the New York World's Fair was opened by President Roosevelt, in whose honour a lunch was given in the Federal Building. The first of the Philharmonic symphony concerts was given under Barbirolli the same evening with Josef Hofmann as soloist.

That month the *Philharmonic Symphony News* announced that " for the first time in over a decade the orchestra will next autumn make an extensive tour of the United States ".

In March—a month before the opening of the World's Fair—the orchestra had gone to Boston to give a concert in Symphony Hall there. Warren Storey Smith, music critic of the *Boston Post*, had written: " The Philharmonic Symphony is to be congratulated in Mr. Barbirolli. . . . In him one now experiences a sense of security, stability, steadfastness, and general satisfaction. . . . Now that his talents have been made known to us, we hope he will in future visit as a guest conductor of the Boston Symphony Orchestra."

In its April 1939 number, *Musical America* reported: " In gratitude for the privilege of singing with the Philharmonic Symphony under John Barbirolli, the two hundred and fifteen members of the Westminster Choir presented to Mr. Barbirolli, after the final performance of the Rossini Mass in Carnegie Hall, a parchment scroll commemorating the performance, signed with the names of the entire choir and Dr. John Finlay Williamson, its leader."

In April, too, the New York Philharmonic Symphony League held its closing event of the 1938–39 season, a luncheon at the Hotel Plaza, at which Barbirolli spoke, with Marshall Field, the president of the orchestra's board of directors, and others. " Barbirolli," said *Musical America*, " pleaded for unstinted devotion to the League and our great orchestra, that the solace of great music might be bequeathed to our descendants."

On May 8th Marshall Field, at the annual meeting of the Philharmonic Symphony Society in the Steinway Hall, announced that " despite the unsettled condition of the World [Hitler had marched into Czechoslovakia] and the recession in business activities in the United States ", the estimated net deficit of 80,000 dollars (about £20,000) for the season had been reduced to 69,000 dollars. The income from the society's endowment fund was decreasing " because of reduced dividends from all securities ", but the income from gramophone recordings and radio had increased. Mr. Field also reported that the attendance at one hundred and four regular subscription concerts in Carnegie Hall was 245,658, or about eighty per cent of the hall's capacity.

During April Barbirolli had taken the orchestra, reduced

to sixty-five players, to Newark, New Jersey, to give a concert before 4,000 people in the city's public hall, the Mosque. " The volatile Barbarolli was seen at his very best," said the *Newark Star Eagle* next morning; adding, " This Barbirolli is a strange, violent, and fascinating character. His actions and gesticulations are wild and eccentric; he fairly breathes every note, every nuance, every shade. He literally ' shakes ' the music from his men and yet he achieves results bordering on the sensational. He was really magnificent in the *Tannhäuser* overture and was cheered to the echo at its conclusion."

Such rhapsodies were common when Barbirolli was on tour. If they were not always marked by musical insight, they were interesting as revealing the impression which Barbirolli made on different types of people. Possibly, too, the orchestra may have let itself go in the Mosque, " to show these provincial boys ". And Barbirolli would merely enter the spirit of the thing. After a gruelling Carnegie Hall season, even a conductor might have his fun away from home. And so to the Hall of Music at the New York World's Fair, with the late Mayor La Guardia conducting the orchestra as a " prelude " to a feast of music.

" Before embarking on the regular programme," said the *New York Times*, " the Philharmonic, the official festival orchestra for the Fair, was heard under the direction of an eminent guest leader, Mayor F. H. La Guardia, who inaugurated the festival with a fanfare for brass instruments composed for this performance by Arcady Debensky, one of the orchestra's second violinists." Then Barbirolli took over the baton from the famous mayor, and the programme proper was played. Earlier in the day the orchestra had given a complete programme at Carnegie Hall, " but they were in praiseworthy form for last night's not unexacting programme at the Fair ".

84

During the summer of 1939 Barbirolli was again in England on vacation. One photograph taken at the time shows him, in gaily striped blazer and a wide-brimmed soft hat, with Parry Jones, the singer. In another photograph he sits mounted on a horse, just setting out for a country ride. But the chief event of his holiday was his marriage to Evelyn Rothwell.

Evelyn was then—and is still—one of the leading oboe players in Britain and had played at the leading desk in the London Symphony and the Scottish orchestras when they were conducted by Barbirolli. On her mother's side she was a descendant of Charles Reade, the novelist. She had taken to the oboe by chance while still at school. There was no one else who knew how to play it, and Evelyn volunteered to try. They got a second-hand oboe sometime before a school concert was due to take place and she played it and liked it. Later she studied with Léon Goossens, and by the time she met Barbirolli, now a famous conductor, she had established herself as an oboist. In the autumn she joined Barbirolli in the United States, and shared his fame and the attention of journalists and Press photographers. One woman journalist, writing for her paper, the *Greensboro Daily News*, from New York, wrote: " One of the few women musicians in history to marry the symphony conductor under whom she played sat quietly in the half-light of a Carnegie Hall box while her husband led the Philharmonic Symphony Orchestra through Elgar's *Introduction and Allegro*. She was the brown-haired, blue-eyed British girl who gave up her career as an oboist when she became the bride of John Barbirolli, because a ' career takes all one's interests and thoughts!' Seldom, if ever before," the writer, Mary Elizabeth Plummer, goes on, " has the venerable Philharmonic had a bride in the conductor's box."

85

The Barbirollis found a home in a suite high up in Hampshire House, which had a superb view of New York's tallest towers. Mrs. Barbirolli was having her first glimpse of America. One of her earliest sensations was to see at dusk the windows of the offices lighting up, one by one. " She was delighted, too," said the indefatigable gossip writer, " with such things as ' the way you wash your hair backward at the hairdresser's ', and ' having olives and celery about all through dinner! ' " But, " foremost in her mind are the warmth of the welcome she received in this country when she finally arrived after several weeks' delay in obtaining passage from London because of the war. Here in New York the orchestra's oboe section hailed her as a friend. The second oboe offered to make her a reed for her instrument. A number of players invited her to play works for oboe and strings with them." The day after that was written the New York Philharmonic's hundred players with the Barbirollis went off on a tour to give fourteen concerts, the tour including Washington, D.C., and Chicago, in the Middle West.

In Washington the *Evening Post*, reporting the arrival of the orchestra, said : " Reporters thought they had met the wrong train when it became apparent that nearly all the passengers were wearing what appeared to be morning clothes—black, broad-brimmed hats and black overcoats. They concluded that was merely the vogue among symphonic musicians this season or that the players were following Mr. Barbirolli's taste in clothes, as they followed his swing of the baton."

There were only two women with the party—Mrs. Barbirolli and Dorle Jarmel, Press representative of the orchestra. It was the first time the orchestra had been in Washington for nine years, and the *Washington Post* said the hundred-and-three musicians, two-thirds of them foreigners, "carried out the most ambitious sightseeing programme since the Postmasters' convention. Violinists, trumpeters, and oboe players tramped through the rain from the White House to the Lincoln Memorial, drove to Mount Vernon and explored Rock Creek Park, before stepping out on the Constitution Hall stage in white tie and tails."

Two thousand people who attended the Thanksgiving concert the same night, November 23, 1939, included most of the *Corps Diplomatique* in Washington and leading members of the capital's society. Constantin Oumansky, the Soviet Ambassador, and his wife were there, and " forty-five members of the United States Marine Band arrived in a body". After the concert there was a supper at Jean's Restaurant, given by the Columbia Broadcasting Company in Mr. and Mrs. Barbirolli's honour.

The next day the orchestra was in Toledo, where, said the *Toledo Times*, " John Barbirolli and his wife Evelyn topped off a two-hour shopping tour of downtown Toledo with a light snack of spaghetti. . . . In the Commodore Perry Hotel lobby he graciously sat down to answer questions, while Mrs. Barbirolli retired to her room. Of his first American concert tour he said: 'We're loving it. Our audiences are showing tremendous enthusiasm.'" Barbirolli, said his interviewer, was wearing his " conservatively-cut " black coat with astrakhan collar and lined with muskrat fur, blue pin-stripe suit, light soft shirt and plain tie, spats and the "customary British black Homburg".

The same minute attention to the conductor's movements were given in the Chicago newspapers when the orchestra visited that great city a day or two later. The playing of the orchestra made a deep impression, the programme including a novelty for Chicago audiences in Weinberger's suite, *Under the Spreading Chestnut Tree*,

composed specially for Barbirolli and first performed at
Carnegie Hall. Elgar's beautiful *Introduction and Allegro*
was also played, with Beethoven's Seventh Symphony and
Berlioz's *Roman Carnival* overture, a work in which the
conductor's and the orchestra's virtuosity was vividly displayed. Richard Bennett, the music critic, wrote of
Barbirolli: " He conducts with an almost mathematical
feeling for phrase length and with a strong sense of the
build-up necessary to have a climax ring true. . . . No wonder
Mr. Weinberger was deeply impressed on hearing part of
his opera *Schwanda* under the leadership of Mr. Barbirolli,
and decided on the spot that ' he had found the ideal
orchestra and the ideal conductor for his new work '. Clear,
concise, uncompromisingly exact, Barbirolli is indeed a conductor any composer would be honoured in having as an
interpreter."

After the concert there was the usual reception, given
this time at their Barton Place home by Mr. and Mrs.
Frederick A. Miller. " The concert was a sell-out and guests
of honour at the reception were the orchestra's famous
conductor, John Barbirolli, and his young British-born
wife," it was said.

And so, on to Columbus, Ohio, where a headline in the
State Journal said; " Capacity audience enthralled by
Barbirolli and 104 men. . . . Concert marks red-letter day
in music here." And then similar rhapsodies in headlines
in Dayton and other American cities included in the tour.
Early in December the orchestra was in Ottawa and Toronto,
in Canada.

At Ottawa Barbirolli and his wife were photographed
with Lord Tweedsmuir (John Buchan), Governor-General,
and Lady Tweedsmuir, at a Government House reception.
That night Lord and Lady Tweedsmuir attended the New
York orchestra's concert at the Capitol Theatre. Right at

the start there was some trouble over late arrivals, which, a writer in the *Ottawa Journal* said, appeared to be a curse of concert-giving in Ottawa. " Promptly as their Excellencies and party entered the Royal box," it was reported, " Mr. Barbirolli stepped to the podium and directed the National Anthem. To his evident amazement a throng of late arrivals were then ushered down the aisles to their seats, making a noise and bustle that prevented the orchestra from going ahead with its first number. Visibly annoyed, Mr. Barbirolli half turned, glared at the offenders, and voiced his indignation to his concert master. He then let his baton drop in despair until the late ones found their seats. . . .

" Speaking to a *Journal* reporter backstage, a member of the orchestra said, ' They wouldn't be allowed to do that in New York; there, the doors are closed just before the concert starts and no one comes in until the interval.' " This same writer observed: " The lobby of the theatre presented a brilliant scene with multi-coloured gowns, luxurious furs, and flashing jewellery of the ladies contrasted with the formal black of their escorts. Watching the audience arrive from the stage door one of the instrumentalists was heard to say, ' They certainly dress up in this city. They're much more formal than our crowds in New York '."

That was in the first week in December. Away in France, Hitler's war had entered what became known as the " phoney " phase. Late in December the orchestra was back in New York, continuing the regular season at Carnegie Hall. Yehudi Menhuin was the soloist in the concert on December 28th, in the Beethoven Violin Concerto. A fortnight later Rachmaninoff played the Beethoven Piano Concerto No. 1 in C major, with the orchestra. In the same programme Barbirolli gave Bruckner's Seventh Symphony. For the next concert the programme consisted of the Bach Fugue in six voices, from *Das Musikalische Opfer* (arranged Howard Ferguson) (played for the first time by the New York orchestra); Violin Concerto in D minor, Brahms (with Mishel Piastro, the leader of the orchestra, as soloist); Classical Symphony, Prokoffief; 'Cockaigne' Overture, Elgar.

CHAPTER IX

VANCOUVER AND CHICAGO

In the first week of February 1940, it was announced in New York that the Philharmonic Symphony Society had re-engaged Barbirolli as conductor for the next two seasons—and that he would be in charge for twenty-two of the thirty weeks' activities planned for 1940–41. Guest conductors engaged for that season were Bruno Walter, then beginning his second guest engagement with the N.B.C. (Toscanini's) Orchestra, and Dimitra Mitropoulos, the forty-four-year-old Greek conductor of the Minneapolis Symphony Orchestra. The London *Daily Telegraph's* New York correspondent cabled home to his paper that "the renewal of Mr. Barbirolli's agreement is a remarkable tribute to the man called upon to succeed Toscanini at the age of thirty-six.... Mr. Barbirolli, whose salary as conductor in New York runs into hundreds of pounds a week, took five-shilling engagements as a 'cellist in London in his early days." During the following week New York had a spate of orchestral music, for apart from the usual Philharmonic Symphony Concert, both the Boston Symphony and the Philadelphia orchestras, with Artur Rubinstein as soloist, visited the city. Barbirolli's programme included the *Merry Wives of Windsor* overture, which moved *Musical America's* critic to remark: "There are, after all, quite a few great orchestral works which Mr. Barbirolli has not given us, so that one wonders a little at his excavation of such pieces as this for his programme, but the audiences love them and that would probably be his answer." Barbirolli's previous programme had consisted of two works by the American composers, Robert L. Sanders (*Little Symphony* in G) and Samuel Barber (*Adagio for Strings*); Shostakovich's suite from the ballet *The Golden Age*; and, for full measure, Tchaikovsky's Piano Concerto in B flat minor, with Simon Barer at the piano. His audiences could therefore scarcely complain of lack of contrast. At the end of February he was giving them a " three B.s " programme: Bach's Brandenburg Concerto No. 3, Beethoven's No. 1 Piano Concerto, and Brahms' First Symphony—Ania Dorfmann being the solo pianist.

About the middle of March the New York orchestra, carrying musical coals to Newcastle, visited Philadelphia for the first time for eight years. It was the first time Philadelphians had seen Barbirolli, and he brought with him for the concert, in the Academy of Music, Helen Traubel, the American Wagnerian soprano from the Metropolitan Opera House, New York. Orchestral works in the programme, apart from the *Die Gotterdammerung* accompaniments to Miss Traubel's arias, were Barbirolli's arrangement of the Purcell suite for strings. Mendelssohn's *Scherzo* in G minor, and Elgar's *Enigma Variations*.

But it was the Wagner music that provided the thrills, and it was said that in this " Mr. Barbirolli reached heights of emotional eloquence and incandescence that quite dwarfed recent performances we have heard here ". In April, back in New York, Barbirolli gave the first performance of Bernard Herrmann's *Moby Dick* cantata for male voices. " Mr. Barbirolli conducted it with superb energy and conviction," wrote Pitts Sanborn, in the *New York World Telegram*. Other items in the same programme were Mozart's *Clemenza di Tito* overture and Haydn's D major Symphony. At the next concert a new *Symphony Concertante*, by Anis Fuleihan, received its first performance.

The evening series of concerts of the orchestra's Carnegie Hall season for 1939–40 concluded on May 1st, and the final concert was given in the afternoon of May 4th. Of the first, Irving Kolodin wrote in the *New York Sun*: " As if to make tacit apology for any sensibilities he might have offended in the past season, John Barbirolli offered an eminently res- pectable programme of symphonic music." This began with Handel's *Concerto Grosso* in B flat, and continued with Mendelssohn's " Italian " Symphony and Sibelius's Second. " Perhaps the most important consequence of the programme," said Kolodin, " was the realization that this Sibelius score has become as much a ' standard ' work as the Handel or Mendelssohn." He added: " There were some discussable aural points in the performance but a more conspicuous feature was visual—the arrangement of the Philharmonic 'cellos and basses at Mr. Barbirolli's right, perhaps for this programme only. In any case the balance of sound was excellent." Olin Downes wrote of the final concert that the works played—Brahms D minor Piano Concerto (with Rudolph Serkin), Smetana's *Bartered Bride* overture, and some Wagnerian excerpts—" were admirably calculated to display as a parting memory the technical and resources of a great orchestra. . . . At the end, conductor and orchestra received hearty applause." After a special concert in New York during the following week, the *World-Telegram* referred to Barbirolli as the " patron saint of overtures ", and went on to say, " Rossini's *Semiramide* is literally a Barbirolli battlehorse. He rides it to panting victory. The throb of it is in his bones."

A few days later Barbirolli arrived with his " charming patrician wife ", as one newspaper called Evelyn, in Canada, to spend a few days in the Rockies before going on to conduct at a concert at Vancouver. Vancouver always gave him a royal welcome and he was fond of performing there, where

Arthur Benjamin, the composer, had settled. *En route*, Barbirolli told Pressmen: "I am ready to trade my baton for a rifle any time my country needs me. I am still a British subject." Then, it was written, "pulling the signet ring off his finger, he said, ' My mother gave me that ring during the last war. I was only seventeen and was with the Suffolk Regiment.'"

Including Vancouver, Barbirolli had arranged to make eighteen appearances as guest conductor during his well-earned holiday. Hollywood and Chicago were also to see him. Before leaving New York he "expressed some challenging opinions concerning the attitude of concert-goers toward new music in general and new music by Americans in particular" in what was called a "back-stage chat" at Carnegie Hall to a few musical journalists. These views are worth giving here in their period context, because they are of universal application and represented Barbirolli's experience in England as well as America. The reserved attitude of the musical public towards "native composers" is not confined to America. "One of the first concerns of a conductor," said Barbirolli, "is, I think, to try to gauge what success has attended his efforts to interest the public in new music. It seems to me that there never has been a time when conductors have sought more diligently for worthy new music to present, and if we do not succeed in finding it, we must confess that the average of production in recent years is below that of the last three or four decades.

"I often ponder with envy the lot my colleagues who were making programmes from 1900 onwards and who were able to introduce to their audiences new works of Richard Strauss, Debussy, Ravel, Stravinsky, Elgar, Delius, and others—works that have since become what we might call modern masterpieces. Having used the word masterpieces, it occurs to me that one of the difficulties to-day is that we

seem to be searching continuously for masterpieces—that
the public wants to hear nothing but masterpieces, with
the result that quite worthy works are sometimes valued at
less than their actual worth. Another question which arises
is ' How curious is the concert-goer to-day? ' When I say
the concert-goer, I don't only mean the American concert-
goer, for I have found by experience in other countries that
curiosity is not one of the more obvious traits of the mass
of the concert-going public. This was brought home to me
recently in a manner which I must admit shocked me at the
time. In the course of a conversation with Mr. Zirato
[Bruno Zirato, assistant manager of the Philharmonic Symphony Society], I heard with almost incredulous astonishment that whenever we announced new American works in
our programme many subscribers asked to have their tickets
changed to the next concerts in which those new works
were not listed. This can only mean one thing—that they
are prepared to damn a new work even before hearing it,
which to say the least is a little premature and unfair. If a
person hears such a work and doesn't like it, he is entitled
to his opinion, but just to stay away when one is programmed
certainly does not help the society or the conductor in their
efforts to give new music its proper chance. I could wish
that more people who are ready to express themselves
vocally and in print on the subject of novelties, both
American and foreign, and who are so quick to criticize
conductors and orchestras for not playing more contemporary works, would lend their support through the box
office when new works are played."

Barbirolli thought there was an explanation of this " lack
of desire for musical experimentation " in the fact that, " we
live in a troubled world, from which it is difficult to find
some release, so perhaps it is not to be wondered at that
people come to music for comfort and refreshment, rather

than with any feeling of duty or desire to explore the paths of contemporary music". Barbirolli goes on: " Nevertheless, analysis of the New York Philharmonic Symphony programmes bears witness that we have not been derelict in our duty to the contemporary composer, American or foreign. And in spite of the lack of curiosity which I have mentioned I still think our duty is very clear. Masterpieces of music are not brought forth every day, but we cannot live entirely in the past, for if we did, we might miss something of the utmost importance."

William G. King, who reported these views in the *New York Sun*, stated that the works of nine living American composers appeared on the season's programmes. *Moby Dick*, by Herrmann, was the " most elaborate, ambitious and expensive novelty of the season," said King, and " most of the critics found it disappointing, and it received a decidedly lukewarm welcome from the public." King recorded that during the same season, works by sixteen living foreign composers were given first performances by Barbirolli and the New York Orchestra. These included works by the British composers, Vaughan Williams, Walton, Bliss, and Britten. " Young Benjamin Britten's violin concerto, which had its first performance anywhere, was probably the most important new work to be introduced by the orchestra during the year. Both critics and audiences gave evidence of liking it." King continues: " It is obvious, therefore, that Mr. Barbirolli and the Philharmonic Symphony Society have indeed done their part in giving the living composer his chance. Twenty-five out of seventy-one composers represented is, it seems to me, a high average. . . . Nine out of seventy-one for Americans is a very fair representation, too, as far as mere figures go. But that brings up another and more important question, one which invites interesting though perhaps painful discussion. And

REHEARSING, EDINBURGH FESTIVAL, 1947

WITH THE HALLÉ ORCHESTRA AT BELLE VUE

that is, ' Were the American works honoured by inclusion in the programmes of the country's oldest orchestra truly representative of the best music being written by contemporary Americans? ' So many considerations must enter into any non-partisan answer to it that this writer, for the moment at least, is not willing to express an opinion. Doubtless others are not only willing and ready but eager to do so." The question put by King was, of course, bound to be asked. It is asked concerning native composers of every other orchestra in every other country in the world. Composers have their partisans, as have conductors, but of Barbirolli it could be said, at least, that he never had any prejudice against American native composers. Indeed, being in a sense, a guest in the United States, he proved the more eager and the more diligent in his search for " native masterpieces ". And, it can be recalled in his favour that a New York critic said of his first season's programmes that " more novelties have been introduced in one season than in a decade under Toscanini ".

The scene changes, and now Barbirolli has reached Vancouver on May 14, 1940 (the time of the great debacle in Europe, with Hitler triumphant). A headline in the Vancouver Daily Province newspaper stated : " John Barbirolli welcomed to city. Brilliant New York conductor met at station by admirers." And Norman Cribbens wrote in the same paper. " John Barbirolli, stocky, dark-eyed little man with the face of a Napoleon and the quick, precise steps of a dancing master, made his bow before an enthusiastic group of admirers gathered to welcome him in the Canadian Pacific station last night. As he stepped from a private compartment, his long black hair slightly awry, his lips parted in a friendly smile, no one guessed twice at his identity. The fine, delicate features and lean expressive hands—sensitized from years of musical experience—quickly identified him as the

G   97

conductor of the New York Philharmonic Symphony Orchestra, renowned for the fire, taste, and intensity of his work."

The background to this reception and adulation was that listeners all over Canada tuned in regularly to the weekly broadcasts of the New York Orchestra over the Columbia system, whose commentators missed no opportunity of " explaining " and describing the conductor. Cribbens continued : " The friendly informality of his handshake revealed him as a brisk and breezy man of the world—easy to meet, easy to like, not difficult to know. But the dogged set of his chin, the purposeful gleam in his eye, seemed to portend many hours of rehearsal for the seventy-nine musicians who will play under Mr. Barbirolli's baton at the concert on Saturday night in aid of the British Columbia Musical Festival."

It was added : " During their stay in Vancouver, the conductor and his wife will occupy a private suite at Hotel Devonshire, where they intend to indulge in their favourite pastime of cooking for themselves."

A day or two later Barbirolli was telling the Vancouverites : " Conductors are born, not made. It is more a matter of feeling than of technical skill. You have to be able to feel what the composer had in mind and convey it to your men by gesture. I am against long explanations at rehearsals. The job is to convey your ideas with your hands, and no amount of musical technique can give you that ability if it doesn't come naturally."

Barbirolli stayed in Vancouver for four days in preparation for a concert with the Vancouver Symphony Orchestra. Each day was occupied with rehearsals which began at 9 o'clock in the morning. Then came Saturday night, the night of the concert, when, in the Forum in Hastings Park, 6,000 people gathered for the occasion. Besides the orchestra of seventy-nine players, there was a choir of seven hundred school children. Arthur Benjamin played the piano part in César Franck's *Symphonic Variations*. The choir sang the "Buchan" version of *O! Canada*, and *God Save the King*, and *Land of Hope and Glory*. And the orchestra played Beethoven's Fifth Symphony and shorter items in a "programme which will be remembered here for a long time to come".

Barbirolli received a tumultuous ovation, a demonstration not unmixed with the "great patriotic fervour aroused by the singing of the national anthems and *Land of Hope and Glory*". And afterwards, "three policemen were needed to hold back the hundreds of school children who swarmed around Mr. Barbirolli's dressing-room seeking his autograph on programmes clutched in eager hands."

This concert—his first in Vancouver—was as inspiring and heart-warming to Barbirolli as to the 6,000 who were in the audience. The date was May 18, 1940.

On his way back to the United States *en route* for Los Angeles to conduct concerts at the Hollywood Bowl, Barbirolli and his wife, "ran into a State Department ruling and were held up at the Canadian border". Reports said that this was "so that the situation arising out of alien restrictions could be ironed out". The ruling insisted that "aliens who leave the United States obtain proper papers before returning". The newspapers reported "Famed conductor comes under these restrictions". But the delay was not long enough to prevent him from arriving in Los Angeles on time, early in July. Barbirolli was also making his début before the great Hollywood (open-air) Bowl audiences with the Los Angeles Philharmonic Orchestra in a "Symphony Under the Stars" programme.

One newspaper writer said: "Conducting Sunday noon broadcasts of the New York Philharmonic for the past five

winters has won John Barbirolli a nation-wide reputation.
His first appearance last night at Hollywood Bowl attracted
the largest attendance on a Friday. Some 12,000 people had
come to hear the English Maestro. . . . They cheered him
when the evening closed with the portentous Brahms E
minor Symphony. Before, they had sat utterly still, for long
moments wrapt in hushed silence, thus paying the most
eloquent tribute that can come to interpreter and music."
Isobel Morse Jones wrote in the Los Angeles Times:
"Hurrah! for Britain. One of her sons smashed through
barriers of propaganda and carefully nurtured ideas of German musical superiority last night in Hollywood Bowl. John
Barbirolli, conducting his second concert in the West,
gave evidence of greatness as a musician and leader of
musicians . . . It was a symphony audience accustomed to
good listening: the concert was deeply satisfying to that
type of audience. . . . The ovation that greeted its finale was
heart-warming for the conductor. The men rose to share it
at his suggestion, but they clapped the conductor right along
with the audience."

One of the items in the programme had been Weinberger's Variations, Under the Spreading Chestnut Tree.
"The whole work is a tribute to England by a man who
never visited there," continued Isobel Morse Jones. "His
admiration for the Elizabethan age, the Madrigalists, the
heroine of Shakespeare's Sonnets, English landscape seen
in pictures at the Louvre, and the Wellers in Pickwick, were
well brought out."

Britain at that moment was a beleaguered country, fighting Hitler alone. . . . It stirred Barbirolli to his depths to find
how warmly American audiences were reacting to anything
English he gave them. And he gave it them often. At the
final concert of the series, Hollywood Bowl was crammed
with 16,000 people, a record. The Hollywood correspondent

of the New York Times wired to his newspaper: "The programme directed by Barbirolli, purely symphonic, not enhanced by the glamour of a stellar singer or virtuoso, stands highest in attendance. There were, no doubt, many radio fans who wanted to see the man Barbirolli after years of hearing him on the air. Los Angeles audiences are 'personality-minded'. Proximity of film stars and film premières have done that. Barbirolli had to be both conductor and star and he succeeded."

During the same season of "outdoor symphony" at Hollywood Bowl, Bruno Walter and Stravinsky were in the list of conductors. Even they did not attract such large audiences. Was this, too, a "tribute to England", fighting for her life, given by many Americans "ninety days to hold out?"

In the last week of July, Barbirolli was in Chicago to conduct the Chicago Symphony Orchestra. After his first concert at Ravinia, Eugene Stinson wrote in the Chicago Daily News: "They say an Englishman dresses for dinner, even when he is going to be served up to cannibals, and at Ravinia on Tuesday evening, when the Chicago Symphony played coatless in the heat, when the rest of us sweltered in the lightest we had, and John Barbirolli, making his début there, preserved immaculate the cuffs of his evening shirt, it seemed inevitable that he should be regarded as a British conductor." Herman Devries, in the Herald American, wrote: "A night such as was last night and a conductor such as is John Barbirolli sufficed fairly to exhaust the thousands that poured into the hot pavilion at Ravinia Park. . . ."

And at the end, "Barbirolli unleashed volleys of plaudits and salvos of bravos and had it not been for the terrific heat, there would have been a stampede at the conclusion". Devries went on: "From the first bars of the overture, The Thievish Magpie, by Rossini, we were riveted in our stall with astonishment at the subtleness and grace with which this aristocrat invested the charming music, but it remained for the Sibelius Symphony No. 2 to make our heart miss a beat and our pulse to throb with an excitement that keyed us up to the burning point."

The Chicago Symphony, at that time under the direction of Frederick Stock, Barbirolli " considered rightly one of the greatest in the world ".

Several other concerts, part of a festival, followed in the Ravinia Pavilion, each inspiring the same rhapsodies in the Press as the first. Summing up, Eugene Devries wrote: " Barbirolli conducts on a more comprehensive basis than any other English conductor we have heard here. He has reserve, yes, but he has not that habitual understatement which Englishmen are prone to bring into even their music."

From Chicago, Barbirolli returned with his wife to Vancouver for a five-weeks holiday until the end of September. They took a house on the North Shore. " Never in any place in the world is there a spot so beautiful as Vancouver. I'm thrilled with it," Mrs. Barbirolli said. Barbirolli's only professional engagement was on September 15th, when he conducted the Vancouver Symphony Orchestra in a concert in aid of the Canadian Red Cross. A picture in the Vancouver Sun about this time shows Barbirolli and his wife sitting on a garden seat, Barbirolli playing his 'cello and Mrs. Barbirolli her oboe. Another picture showed them " studying the score of a new symphony ". They saw much of Arthur Benjamin during this stay and Benjamin composed for Mrs. Barbirolli the concerto for orchestra and oboe in which she has since been heard in performances in Britain. In October, the New York Philharmonic Symphony Orchestra's 1940–41 season started.

CHAPTER X

CENTENARY AND A TRIP HOME

ONE of the features of the first part of the New York Orchestra's 1940–41 season was a special concert which Barbirolli devoted to the works of Sibelius, in honour of the composer's seventy-fifth birthday. One critic wrote: " The English conductor is fast becoming a Sibelian of commanding stature."

Barbirolli sent greetings to Jean Sibelius, and some time later the composer replied: " My dear Master: Please accept my heartfelt thanks for your friendly thoughts and kind congratulations . . . I wish to thank you from my heart for all that you have done for me and my music. I am always glad when my works are in your masterful hands. . . . Jean Sibelius."

During the first week in December, Barbirolli and the orchestra visited Boston and Springfield, Mass. For the Boston concert Barbirolli introduced his orchestration of Purcell's Chaconne in G minor, which American audiences had not yet heard.

" I believe " said Barbirolli on arrival in Boston, " this work, which lasts ten minutes, will be a revelation of the genius of the great English composer. It will show that three hundred years ago he was making a masterly use of such a supposedly twentieth century device as atonality. The music is extremely beautiful and shows great resourcefulness of invention. Beauty is uppermost, however. In listening, one loses sight of the fact that it is an amazing technical feat.

Probably I shall be accused by critics of taking liberties with the composition written three centuries ago by Purcell. But the strikingly modern chromaticism is his. My work was simply to transcribe the Chaconne, which is for viols alone, so as to enable its possibilities to be realized more fully by the audiences of to-day, by the use of woodwind and four horns, in addition to the strings."

The original manuscript of this Purcell work was discovered in Glasgow and Barbirolli had made his orchestral arrangement during his holidays the previous summer. Apparently the Boston audience endorsed his own feelings about the beauty of the work.

On December 17, 1940, Barbirolli and his wife left New York for a ten-days' holiday in the Finger Lake region. There was a break in the Philharmonic Symphony Season until February 13, 1941, and after his Christmas holiday, Barbirolli undertook engagements in the West. On December 29th and January 5th he directed the Ford Symphony Hour broadcasts in Detroit. On January 10th he conducted the San Francisco Symphony Orchestra in its home city, after which he was in charge at a series of seven concerts given by the Los Angeles Philharmonic.

The Battle of Britain had been fought and won. Given " ninety days ", Britain had survived. But raids on London were proceeding with all their fury, causing Barbirolli not a little anxiety about his relatives. Nearly another year had to run before Pearl Harbour and before the black-out and war tension were to descend on the Pacific coast.

Barbirolli's arrival in the " Southland " was marked by the usual fanfares in the Press. Receptions were arranged in his honour. In Los Angeles he was asked for his views on some remarks by Sir Thomas Beecham (then, and for most of the war, in the United States) on " films and music ". The Los Angeles Times said: " Motion pictures, maligned in the sphere of music, to-day had a champion. He is John Barbirolli, conductor of the New York Philharmonic Symphony Orchestra. . . . He questions the remarks of Sir Thomas Beecham, also a conductor, who recently said, ' the cinema falsifies all values ', and that the motion pictures made ' music a shocking noise '. Barbirolli declared: ' The truth is that practically all the world's leading modern composers have contributed to motion-picture music, and are at present contributing '.

" He named Ernest Toch, who wrote ' Big Ben ', which he [Barbirolli] will conduct here, Milhaud, Arthur Bliss, Korngold, Benjamin Britten, Zador, and others. Barbirolli continued, ' Motion pictures, radio and phonograph records, all referred to as canned music, have all played their part in heightening interest in both the symphony and opera. They are therefore allies to musicians, and are, in a sense, responsible for their bread and butter. I have conducted for phonograph records and I am proud of the fact. I have also many friends in motion-picture work who are doing excellent work '."

The next day the same newspaper announced that Jack L. Warner, vice-president in charge of production at Warner Bros' Studios, had been chosen as a member of the Southern California Symphony Association's board of trustees. This association sponsored the winter concerts of the Los Angeles Philharmonic Orchestra and the summer series at Hollywood Bowl of " Symphonies Under the Stars ".

Apart from the San Francisco and Los Angeles concerts, Barbirolli during 1941 conducted in San Diego, Claremont, and on the University of Southern California campus. Two " premières " in Los Angeles were Toch's *Big Ben*, a " variation-fantasy " on the Westminster Chimes and Bizet's First Symphony, the only symphonic work of Bizet's to reach the orchestral repertoire. Toch composed his work after a visit to London. He was now living in Los Angeles and a member of the South California music faculty.

On January 24th, Barbirolli conducted the Los Angeles orchestra in the Passadena Civic Auditorium, with Heifetz as soloist. He returned to New York in February and towards the end of that month had Rachmaninoff as soloist in Rachmaninoff's *Rhapsody on a theme of Paganini* for piano and orchestra. Another work in the same programme was Sibelius's *Pelleas et Melisande* suite, a work new to America and composed in 1905, three years after Debussy's opera was produced. Pitts Sanborn in the *New York World Telegram* wrote of this concert, " At the end, the audience thundered its approval ".

During the first week in March, a new work by Italo Montemezzi, based on Saint-Pierre's *Paul et Virginie*, was given in Carnegie Hall, with the composer as guest conductor, and at the next concert several works by American composers were introduced. These included orchestral interludes from Roy Harris's " Folk Song " Symphony. This was at the Thursday and Sunday concerts and the programme contained only one familiar work, the Schumann piano concerto, Beveridge Webster playing the solo part. Of this concert, devoted mainly to " novelties " by American composers, the *New York Sun* reported: " Vacant seats at Sunday afternoon concerts of the Philharmonic Symphony have been blamed on sunny weather, that lures subscribers and others to the country. That could scarcely have been the right explanation yesterday, when a mostly American programme was played by John Barbirolli's ensemble. This time there was the slush of Friday's heavy snow to deter those who may not have been completely convinced in advance of the audience-appeal of the unfamiliar music they had opportunity to consider. Interest in the American works played was mostly of an order that may be termed ' professional '.

Fellow American composers had opportunity to analyse and compare works of three of their number "—Roy Harris, Morton Gould, and Bernard Wagenaar—" as different as they were representative. But presumably what a greater number of the audience remembered when they left the hall was an able, if scarcely remarkable, performance of the Schumann concerto."

So the season proceeded, with Barbirolli tactfully varying the classical programmes with works modern and not so modern, American as well as British and Continental. As has already been said, it could never be said that he neglected the American composer. Had he not been so sensitive about their claims, the box office might have shown even better results. It is a melancholy fact that in America, as in Britain, modern works by native composers are not taken kindly by average audiences. Barbirolli neglected no opportunity of trying to break this attitude down in America, but with small success.

A little later, on March 12th, the concert in Carnegie Hall was in memory of Pitts Sanborn, whom we have quoted several times, and who had died a few days previously. Besides being a music critic, he had been writing the programme notes for the Philharmonic Symphony for many years, and the programme was prefaced with one of his favourite pieces, the *Prelude Religioso* from Rossini's *Messe Solonelle*. At the same concert New York heard for the first time Villa Lobos's symphonic suite, *Discobrimento do Brazil*. It was received with great enthusiasm. The programme ended with the Brahms D minor Piano Concerto, Artur Rubinstein being the soloist.

Before the month was out Barbirolli introduced a symphony (also new to Carnegie Hall) by Eugene Goossens, the British composer-conductor who had been conducting the Cincinnati Orchestra. Goossens was present and heard his work applauded, and bowed from the platform. This was Goossens' opus 58, and he began it on his forty-fifth birthday, in May 1938. He had worked on it, he said, in London and Paris and at sea, and it was first played by the Cincinnati Orchestra, to which it was dedicated, in April 1940. Francis Perkins wrote in the *New York Herald Tribune*: "There is a plenitude of musical ideas and of thematic material in the four movements and forty minutes of the work. . . . There are some vague reminiscences but the work gives a sense of individuality of style, rather than of eclecticism."

Jose Iturbi also took part in the programme which introduced the new Goosens symphony, so that there were, as the newspapers remarked, "three conductors, all in a row". But Barbirolli was the only one who conducted. Iturbi played the Tchaikovsky B flat minor concerto.

The early summer saw Barbirolli again "hitting the headlines" in Los Angeles, with the Los Angeles Philharmonic. He had become an established favourite there, not only because he was conductor of the New York Philharmonic Symphony, but also "for the things he does to us, musically," as one listener said.

There is no doubt that he enjoyed these engagements in California as much as the audience there enjoyed his concerts. One memorable concert during that August of 1941 was one at which Helen Traubel—making her début at the Bowl—sang Wagner arias, and the Metropolitan opera star received, with Barbirolli, a frantic ovation. Rain fell on the Bowl at Barbirolli's final concert. It was the first time this had happened for three years and only once had it been sufficient to interfere with a performance, when a ballet was postponed. On this occasion, "the audience of 7,000 made it clear that its ardour had not been dampened otherwise than to cause an effervescence of appreciation for Barbirolli's farewell performance here."

But it was only to be farewell for the summer. In November Barbirolli was back again, that is to say, after the New York season of 1942–43 had resumed, and it was reported: " Members of the Women's Committee of the Philharmonic Orchestra in Los Angeles launched their regular luncheon series on November 18th, with John Barbirolli, conductor, and Vladimir Horowitz, soloist, at the opening concert as guests. . . ."

It may be remarked, incidentally, what an important part these Women's Committees played in the affairs of every big orchestra in America. This was, and is, perhaps, typical of all forms of social and cultural activity in the United States. It has often been of invaluable assistance in maintaining good relations between an orchestra and the public, and if there were more of it in Britain, some of our orchestras might the more easily solve their problems. It has, however, disadvantages.

About this time in Los Angeles, a special concert was given in aid of a Russian medical relief campaign (Russia having, the previous June, been attacked by Hitler) and the concert was notable for the fact that both Horowitz and Heifetz appeared as soloists, with Barbirolli conducting the Los Angeles Orchestra. All the musicians " gave " their services.

In December Barbirolli was again in Vancouver, guest-conductors occupying the podium at Carnegie Hall, where the December " recess " was also near. He had spent part of his summer holidays on the North Shore and a picture of him in a Vancouver newspaper bore the caption: " Home again ". The newspaper reported: " The conductor is renewing acquaintance with many a friend . . . and seeing again the scenery he calls the world's finest." Then followed a series of concerts with the Vancouver Symphony Orchestra, many of whose players called him a " miracle-worker ", because " he brings music out of us we did not know was there ".

In February 1942 Barbirolli was conducting in Seattle and in Cincinnati, Goossens' " field ". He made a deep impression at Cincinnati. Frederick Yeisen wrote in *The Cincinnati Enquirer*: " There is nothing like a change of diet. It works in music, too, with conductors. John Barbirolli, having swapped pulpits for a concert or two with Eugene Goossens, had an invigorating affect on the atmosphere in Music Hall yesterday. Both the members of the Cincinnati Symphony Orchestra and the public reacted to Mr. Barbirolli's direction like a tonic. . . . He creates the illusion of playing on the orchestra as though it were an instrument, instead of merely leading it. . . . What he also did was to brighten up the tone of the orchestra." Barbirolli stayed in Cincinnati for two weeks, and then returned to New York to resume his direction of the Philharmonic Symphony.

This was gala time with the orchestra, which was celebrating its centenary. Seven hundred people, among them scores of famous musicians, attended a centenary reception at Steinway Hall, the orchestra's headquarters, given by Mrs. Theodore Steinway in honour of Barbirolli and the orchestra. " Mr. Barbirolli cut an enormous cake decorated with a model of the full orchestra in concert position." Telegrams of congratulation " poured in " and much was written about the hundred years history of the orchestra. But the chief feature of the centenary was the galaxy of guest-conductors, headed by Toscanini, who came forward to conduct some of the concerts.

The event was somewhat overshadowed by the fact that America was now in the war and girding her loins, but it also served to show that music was among things eternal and particularly that the orchestra had survived other wars, to reach even greater heights. The anniversary concert itself was in the hands of Barbirolli and one of the works in the programme was his own transcription of Bach's chorale-prelude, *Wenn wir in Hoechstein Noethen Sind*, dictated by Bach " almost with his last breath ".

In the early summer of 1942, at the end of the centenary season, Barbirolli was on his way home. From the beginning of the war he had longed to see his family and friends, and to make some contribution himself to Britain's effort. The worse things looked, the more anxious he became. He was receiving letters from home which told him of the revival of music and of the struggles most orchestras were going through to meet the demand. It was then that he formed the idea of helping by offering to give up his ten weeks' holiday to visit England at his own expense, giving his services to any orchestra that cared to use them. Transport difficulties were serious, but the then First Lord, Mr. A. V. Alexander, an old friend of Barbirolli's, and a passionate lover of music, informed him that if he cared to risk the hazards attending trans-Atlantic crossings—the U-boat menace was at its peak —arrangements could be made.

The upshot was two concerts for the Royal Philharmonic Society, a tour of England with the London Symphony Orchestra, and a tour of England and Scotland with the London Philharmonic—whirlwind tours, with a concert nearly every day or evening. He would have liked to stay longer, but there was the journey back, and all its perils to be faced. Of his ten weeks' vacation, some seven weeks were spent at sea on the way here and returning to America.

Barbirolli came over in a 3,000-ton Norwegian freighter, the *California Express*. After a hazardous and exciting voyage he reached Liverpool after twenty-three days.

" I feel I shall always think that my arrival in my native land at that time was one of the most wonderful moments of my life," he told the writer recently. " I could not help but feel sad at all the ravages I saw, but the wonderful feeling of confidence and discipline, and what, for want of a better term, we will call ' guts ' will ever be memorable."

The welcome he received at his first concert (at the Cambridge Theatre with the London Symphony Orchestra) made him feel that it was more than worth while coming over, " even if he never got back ". The two concerts in the Royal Albert Hall took place before audiences of between 7,000 and 10,000, and Barbirolli also wound up the London Musical Festival held during that summer. Before he left England the L.S.O. presented him with a silver cigarette box, and the L.P.O. gave him two elegantly bound volumes of Beethoven's " Ninth " and " Tristan ".

Eventually came the day for departure—this time in a small Fyffe banana boat taking back some crews who were to take over ships on the other side. Among these, says Barbirolli, were " two wonderful old chief engineers, both over seventy, who had emerged from retirement to perform this most hazardous task ". The voyage was even more exciting than the homeward one and the ship fell among a submarine pack soon after sailing with the convoy. Even so, the journey took a day less—twenty-two days, against twenty-three days—than that of the Norwegian freighter which had brought the conductor home.

When he reached Los Angeles in September (before the opening of his last New York season) he told one hundred members of the Women's Committee, " how the old country was doing ". He declared that " although thousands of homes [in Britain] have been destroyed, and many lives have been lost, the British people have the will and determination to carry on until victory has been won." The report added, " He declared that people of this nation [U.S.A.] are whimpering because of slight inconveniences, not realizing sacrifices other war-torn nations were making. . . . His views

[The Nottingham Journal Ltd.

JOHN BARBIROLLI WITH JOHN WOOLFORD, HIS FORMER
PERSONAL SECRETARY IN NEW YORK, AND
LAURANCE TURNER, LEADER OF THE HALLÉ ORCHESTRA

MR. AND MRS. BARBIROLLI ON HOLIDAY IN THE
COTSWOLDS

were received with enthusiasm by the audience, as they brought to mind the conditions existing in the British Isles and the faith and courage of the British people." Emil Ludwig spoke at the same meeting.

Principal 'cellist of the Los Angeles Orchestra was Lauri Kennedy, who had been with the B.B.C. orchestra in London before going to America, and at the first concert which Barbirolli conducted Kennedy played the solo part in the Saint-Saëns concerto. Barbirolli's engagement at Los Angeles was for three months and during that time he conducted at many concerts, always crowded, arranged for American troops, airmen and naval men, said to be " gasping for good music ". The final concert, said the newspaper reports, "featured an all-Tchaikovsky programme, with Artur Rubinstein as soloist; and John Barbirolli, as conductor, was awarded the cup for the largest attendance of the year ".

CHAPTER XI

INVITATION FROM THE HALLÉ

The year 1943 was to be the most momentous of all at this stage of Barbirolli's career. His visit to his homeland the previous year had accentuated his homesickness. The overpowering impressions he had received during his whirl-wind tour of England, and the warm and unmistakable esteem manifested towards him by the British public, worked on his mood. And although he had had to leave England at the end of this tour to honour his contracts in America, he knew he would soon have a big decision to make. As it happened, events moved quickly. In March 1943, he gave his last concert with the New York Philharmonic. In April the world heard the news of his appointment as Music Director of the Hallé Orchestra. But this is to anticipate.

Barbirolli returned to New York early in 1943, and in his February programme he introduced Vaughan Williams's " Pastoral " Symphony, of which Olin Downes wrote in the *New York Times*: " For me this symphony is one of abiding poetry, singularly personal and independent in its craftsmanship and unique in its evocation of beauty. We find few symphonies so individual in mood and manner and so integrated in the working out of ideas. It is musical procedure which is not according to stock formulas, but an organic growth consequent upon the inner dynamic of the themes. . . . The tenor voice back of the stage which preludes and concludes the last movement . . . seems a voice of nature."

The programme opened with a "thunderous burst", when the orchestra gave the first New York performances of Llewellyn Gower's transcription for many instruments of the *Introduction and Fugue* of Bach's unaccompanied 'cello sonata in C minor. The programme of another concert during February consisted chiefly of unfamiliar scores by living composers. Fritz Kreisler played in the same programme in his Concerto in C major for violin, string orchestra and organ in the manner of Antonio Vivaldi, a work which Barbirolli had found much pleasure in studying with Kreisler.

Kreisler closed the concert with a "stunning" performance of the Viotti Violin Concerto in A minor, "playing it like the great master he is".

From now on the Carnegie Hall audience began to see soloists in uniform, among them Sergeant Eugene List and Corporal Edward Kilyeni, of the Army Air Forces. Kilyeni appeared in Barbirolli's last New York concert, on March 7th, playing the Liszt Piano Concerto in E flat. The orchestral works in the programme were Tchaikovsky's Fifth Symphony and Lucien Caillet's *Fantasia and Fugue on Oh, Susannah*, described by a critic as "elaborate in texture and replete with bells" and suggesting "the musical background for a feature-length 'Mickey Mouse' or, possibly, 'Snow White'." At the end of the concert, after many minutes of applause, both audience and orchestra sang *Auld Lang Syne*.

A week later, Barbirolli was once more in Vancouver, where he conducted the Vancouver Symphony Orchestra in a programme which included works by Weber, Holst, Debussy, Tchaikovsky and Beethoven. The next morning Stanley Bligh wrote in the *Vancouver Sun*: "The players presented a performance that had fewer technical imperfections than any concert in the society's history. The precision, clarity of tone . . . were evidence of the conductor's teaching skill."

In the following month Barbirolli's appointment as permanent conductor of the Hallé Orchestra was announced in the United States and Canadian newspapers. One of the American musical journals made the announcement under the heading, "Our loss, Manchester's gain," and recalled the great history of the Hallé. Alice Brewer wrote a two-column article about the British orchestra's history and Barbirolli's new job, in a New York daily. "The news that John Barbirolli is to take over the conductorship of the great Hallé Orchestra, of Manchester, England, will come as no surprise to the admirers of this singularly magnetic personality. To be invited to the permanent conductorship of the famous Hallé Orchestra means that Barbirolli is acknowledged to be one of the few great conductors in the world by those who are competent to judge. His career has been meteoric. . . . He will know his dish well and not expect the electric atmosphere of New York. It is certain he will meet many old friends there who will gladly welcome him as one returning home, unspoiled by his halo of success. All music lovers will wish him well."

Another American newspaper, reporting that the Hallé were embarking on one all-the-year-round season, declared: "That's British determination for you! "

The Vancouver Sun for April 12, 1943, reprinted in its entirety an article from the London Observer, headed "Barbirolli–Hallé Era," which ended with the words: "Manchester will be proud to have him and one can safely predict a splendid future for ' Barbirolli with the Hallé '."

The Musical America magazine mentioned that the committee of the Hallé Society, in issuing the invitation, said that "they feel convinced that your acceptance would mean the beginning of a new and glorious era for the Hallé".

This phrase was part of the letter written to Mr. Barbirolli by Philip Godlee, chairman of the committee.

Barbirolli's own views were expressed in an interview with Hessel Tiltman, New York Correspondent of Kemsley Newspapers. "Before I had read to the end of the invitation I knew my answer," said Barbirolli ". . . The whole thing was fixed up within two weeks. And here I am, feeling very proud and happy to be allowed to make my contribution to British music at this time." He looked back over his career, and continued: "These years in the U.S.A. have produced their memories, too. I have given one-hundred-and-forty first-performances of all kinds over here. One of my most thrilling experiences this side of the Atlantic was a performance of Delius's *On hearing the First Cuckoo in Spring*, played on a perfect summer's night in Hollywood Bowl to 15,000 people listening in perfect silence. Another American memory I will always treasure was when, at the end of my final concert in New York, after many minutes of applause, when I had said a few words about, 'There has come an end to my seven years here', both audience and orchestra rose and sang *Auld Lang Syne*. Nor will I ever forget the loyalty and affection I have received from New York audiences all these years."

Barbirolli then went on to speak of his future plans. "I am going to Manchester with a completely open mind," he said. "I am inclined to think it will be a good thing to decentralize a bit and play in all districts around the city. . . . The great thought in my mind is that, guided by my great predecessors, Hallé, Richter, Ballin, and Harty, I hope to make the future of the Hallé as worthy and as great as its past. If from this side of the Atlantic I may intrude my opinion on any aspect of orchestral music, I would like to say just this—I have noticed a tendency on both sides of the Atlantic for the public to flock always to hear the old favourites and it is still a great problem for a conductor and his management to play much new or experimental music without danger of serious financial loss. Of course this tendency can be largely explained at the present time by the fact that in these days people mostly go to concerts after a hard day's work, seeking relaxation. But it is hoped that, with more normal times, there will come a return of musical curiosity. It is good for conductor, orchestra, and audience to tread new paths and so avoid becoming stale through constant repetition."

He concluded by paying tribute to " my old friend " Sir Hamilton Harty, who had died in 1941; " During his period the Hallé reached heights that have certainly never been surpassed," he said. " The greatest satisfaction is the opportunity given to me by Manchester to participate in what I confidently believe to be a new and memorable chapter now opening in British orchestral music."

Fittingly enough, Barbirolli's last concert on the American continent was at Vancouver, for that " near English " city had been home to him during his years in America. After seven years as conductor of the New York Philharmonic (a term of office only once exceeded—by Toscanini) he now looked towards England, home, and duty.

CHAPTER XII

BRITAIN'S OLDEST ORCHESTRA

In accepting the conductorship of the Hallé Barbirolli was again linking his name with an established orchestra with a permanent home and a tradition to maintain. Manchester, indeed, had the only orchestra in Britain which could make an offer that was sufficiently attractive to enable him to return home. The London Philharmonic and London Symphony Orchestras were, and are still, without permanent conductors. Neither of these orchestras could have offered the same scope to a conductor of Barbirolli's standing.

In the case of the Hallé, however, the term "permanent home" had by 1943 become of doubtful significance. The Free Trade Hall, where for nearly ninety years the weekly Hallé concerts had been held, had been all but destroyed in the blitz of December 1940, and still remains a shell. But the tradition remained.

After Hamilton Harty gave up the post of permanent conductor in 1933, his place had not been filled, but regular seasons had been carried out under various conductors, notably Beecham and Sargent. In the end the committee decided upon the bold stroke of reconstituting the orchestra on a full-time, yearly-contract basis and offering the conductorship to Barbirolli at a salary which was higher than that of any other conductor in Britain.

At the time, most of the Hallé players were also members of the B.B.C. Northern Orchestra, an arrangement that had been in existence for some time. This had created divided loyalties which were satisfactory to neither orchestra, and it was decided to give all the players the choice of either accepting full-time contracts with the Hallé Orchestra or joining the B.B.C. The result was that all but a brilliant nucleus of twelve, including Laurance Turner, the leader, Haydn Rogerson, principal 'cello, Pat Ryan, first clarinet, and the veteran harpist, Charles Collier, who had played under Richter, chose to join the B.B.C. Barbirolli was thus left with the task of building up what was almost entirely a new orchestra, with the name, tradition and historical background of the old Hallé.

The original orchestra was formed when Charles Hallé, born in Hagen, Westphalia, in 1819, accepted the conductorship of the Gentlemen's Concerts in Manchester.[1] These concerts had been begun in 1774 and continued uninterruptedly until 1920.

Hallé was the son of a Lutheran organist and made his first public appearance as a pianist when he was seven under the wing of Louis Spöhr. The performance was a success, but Hallé was taken back by his father for a further seven years' study, being allowed to make one annual appearance to show the townspeople how much progress he was making.

At the age of 17, in 1836, he went to Paris, where his gifts ripened rapidly and he met Chopin, Liszt, Paganini, Cherubini, Berlioz, and Wagner. He lived and worked in Paris for twelve years and became known to the musical public as a brilliant performer and sensitive musician. To the Paris public he is said to have introduced the Beethoven Sonatas, all of which he played from memory. He also established there a regular series of chamber-music concerts, although few of his friends expected them to succeed.

---

[1] I am indebted to Mr. John F. Russell, Librarian of the Henry Watson Music Library, for most of the facts given in this chapter. Extracts quoted are from Mr. Russell's *Historical Outline of the Hallé Concerts.*

For composers and musicians who were acquiring world-wide reputation, the Paris of that time was the ideal retreat. Arts and letters and political philosophy flourished throughout a dazzling decade, and all seemed right with the world. Soon, however, the political atmosphere grew dark and tense, and the revolution of 1848 broke out. Many artists and idols of the salons were implicated on the wrong side, and Hallé, with others, found at last that life in the French capital had become too uncongenial for creative work.

He had been offered the post of French Ambassador to the German Diet at Frankfort. Since he was presumably still a German subject, this offer seems to have been regarded as a tribute to Hallé's political integrity, as well as to his popularity in high circles. But a diplomatic career held no attraction for him, and he left France and went to London. There he scored an immediate success in Beethoven's *Emperor Concerto* at a concert at the Covent Garden Theatre, and was promptly engaged by John Ella, a Yorkshire-born impresario, for the concerts of the Musical Union. Ella established these concerts in London, and engaged famous Continental artists for them, and also enabled them to tour the provinces: he was also the first to introduce programme notes.

Hallé paid his first visit to Manchester during August 1848 and attended a Gentlemen's Concert at which Chopin played. That night, too, Hallé met the Irish pianist George Osborn, from whom he had taken lessons in Paris. Osborn was the accompanist in the concert programme. There was also in Manchester another man whom Hallé had known in Paris, Herman Leo, a Manchester calico printer, and it was Leo who in the end persuaded Hallé to " give Manchester a trial ", and to take charge of the Gentlemen's Concerts, in 1849.

Hallé made one condition which had far-reaching consequences. It was that he should be allowed to reorganize " the band ", whose performances he found well below London or Continental standards. No longer, he decided, would the double basses be ranged in a row in the forefront of the orchestra, as they were when he first saw them. Hallé retained the best of the players in the existing orchestra and filled the vacant places by bringing seasoned professionals from London and the Continent, a leavening that put a different complexion on all future performances. Mr. Russell says, indeed, that " the result of the reorganization so astounded the subscribers that they were ready to agree to anything ". Thus began seriously the " cultivation of orchestral music in Manchester ", and while it was Hallé's chief concern thereafter, he did not neglect chamber music. In time he began to go farther afield and formed a link between Liverpool and the Hallé players that outlasted his own time. The first musical event he gave Liverpool was a Chamber Concert. There were only eleven people in the audience, four of them reporters!

In 1852 Hallé was invited to conduct the St. Cecilia Society, which had been newly formed in Manchester for the study of choral works. With a mixed choir of fifty voices he made the Society's concerts a success, until he could no longer spare the time for them and handed over the con-ductorship to Edward Hecht, who had settled in Manchester in 1854 and died there in 1887, after becoming chorus-master and deputy-conductor of the Hallé.

Much of Hallé's success in Manchester was due to the interest taken in his musical ventures by the cosmopolitan colony of business-men and amateur musicians then living in the city. One of his most devoted admirers was Frederick Engels, the collaborator and financial backer of Karl Marx, who lived in Manchester for twenty years until he retired from the family cotton business of Ermon and Engels, in

1870. Julius Delius, the father of the composer and a friend of Engels, was the leader of a group of Bradford business-men from whom Hallé always received powerful support for his orchestra. Another man to stand out in the early lists of Hallé's supporters was that of Gustav Behrens, whose descendants have continued to play a decisive part in the Hallé Society's affairs.

In 1857 Manchester held a great exhibition of art treasures, and Hallé had been given the task of providing music "worthy of the occasion". He was, says Mr. Russell, " not satisfied merely to put in the Gentlemen's Concerts orchestra for this purpose, but invited a number of players from London and the Continent. The result was an exceptionally fine and well-balanced orchestra of a hundred players, to which was allied a specially built organ . . . afterwards removed to the Free Trade Hall."

At the concerts which Hallé gave with this orchestra during the Art Treasures Exhibition, " symphonies of the finest classical composers, Beethoven, Haydn, and Mozart, which had hitherto been confined to the more or less select audiences of the concert halls, were made familiar to a wide audience. Even if they were leavened with operatic selections, nevertheless they must have made a vast impression on the many thousands who stayed to listen."

The exhibition was visited by Queen Victoria and by people from all over the country. The Free Trade Hall had been built, and on the evening of the opening day of the exhibition Hallé gave a great concert there, with choir and orchestra, Hallé himself playing in the *Emperor Concerto*. Mr. Russell records that Clara Novello, Mrs. Lockley, and Sims Reeves were soloists in this concert.

So great was the success of the exhibition orchestra that Hallé was emboldened at the beginning of the following year to launch a series of weekly concerts " at his own risk ".

The first year he made a tiny profit which, says Mr. Russell, " was presented to him in solemn state by Mr. Forsyth in the form of ten bright, new threepenny bits. One for each member of the family—less than twopence a concert; but sufficient to persuade him to try another season. And so the Hallé Concerts, so boldly launched, went on."

The original account books, written in Hallé's own hand, show that four years later, in 1862, the profits had grown to £1,228 and four years after that to £2,000.

Hallé seems to have played solos or in concertos at most of his concerts. For the choral work he had the fully-trained choir of 250 of the Manchester Choral Society, founded about 1830. Joachim played at the fifteenth concert of the series in the Mendelssohn concerto. Mr. Russell declares that in the two first seasons (the second consisted of 27 concerts) eight Beethoven symphonies were played, four of Mozart's, four of Haydn's, and two of Mendelssohn's.

For the rest, the programmes were sometimes on the popular side. But late in his life, Hallé prided himself on the number of those he called " artisans " attending his concerts, and he claimed that even among these a love for severely classical music had grown up. A large proportion of the Free Trade Hall seats could be had for a shilling. This hall held twice as many as the old Gentlemen's Concerts Hall.

" By this time " (round about 1858 says Mr. Russell), " Manchester's first resident professional orchestra was fully established, and orchestral concerts took the place formerly held by choral concerts and performances by visiting (largely foreign) celebrities. In this development there was all the difference musically between an occasional snack and regular full-size meals. The public preferred the more solid fare."

In 1858 Hallé's orchestra consisted of sixty players led by A. C. Seymour, a local violinist of repute who had been leader and conductor of the Gentlemen's Concerts before Hallé's time. Seven of the first violins were imported from London, Paris, and Liverpool. Only one of the ten second violins and one of the six viola players were imported. Four of the five 'cellos were supplied by London, Paris, and Leicester. It was the well-known Vieuxtemps who came from Paris to lead them. Most of the woodwind and brass were local players, but Raspi, the first bassoon, came from Turin. Later, an oboist, Eugl, came from Vienna to join the orchestra. During the 1861 season, Jenny Lind sang in Haydn's *Creation* with Sims Reeves and Belletti in Manchester, and sang at the regular Hallé concert the next night. The " Swedish Nightingale " sang twice with Hallé during the following season.

By 1865 Hallé had increased his orchestra to eighty players. In 1873, after Bach's *St. Matthew Passion* had been performed for the first time in Manchester, Joachim played, with Madame Neruda, Bach's Double Concerto in D minor at a special concert. Madame Neruda, herself a celebrated violinist in her own right, later became Lady Hallé. In 1889 Edward Grieg conducted the orchestra at one concert, while Hallé played his piano concerto. And Madame Grieg sang. Mr. Russell tells how, according to a man who attended that concert, Hallé had asked Grieg to play the piano part in his concerto himself, but Grieg declined, saying: " I do not play well enough for Manchester."

Thus, forty years after he had got together his orchestra for the Art Treasures Exhibition, and six years before his death, Hallé could look upon the results of his work in Manchester with considerable satisfaction. He had created an orchestra equal, perhaps, to any heard in London, and had also made the name of Manchester as famous in the musical as in the commercial world. For forty years the Hallé Orchestra's concerts had been in his own hands, and during the early part of the period it had been known as " Mr. Hallé's band ". " He raised the orchestra " said one writer, " to a pitch of perfection unknown at that time."

Hallé married Madame Normann Neruda, then forty-nine years old, in 1888. She was the widow of a Ludwig Normann and daughter of Josef Neruda, whose family had long been famous for producing first-rate musicians. In the year of his marriage Hallé was knighted and in 1890 and 1891 he toured with his wife in Australia and elsewhere. He died in Manchester on October 25, 1895. In 1896 a public subscription was raised for Lady Hallé, under Royal patronage and in 1901 Queen Alexandra gave her the title of " violinist to the Queen ". She " was the first of the women violinists who could stand comparison with the men," it was said.

It would be almost impossible to give any estimate of Hallé as a conductor in terms of our own age of virtuoso conductors. Nor would anything be gained by it. Hallé's monument rested in the fact that the concerts as he left them formed the pattern of all future events. He established a tradition which has been handed down almost intact to our own day. And that is a thing that can be said only of two or three orchestras in the whole world.

After Hallé's death the question of forming some organization for continuing the orchestral concerts became urgent. It had, in fact, been discussed by Hallé during his lifetime with Mr. Gustav Behrens and others, Hallé having, as Mr. Russell says, " a horror lest they should fall into the hands of some impressario solely concerned about profits ". A meeting had been convened in Manchester Town Hall in 1891 to " consider the formation of a Society to take over the concerts and carry on the same artistic policy ".

It was at this meeting also that the idea of founding a college of music in Manchester was launched; Hallé was the prime mover in this enterprise and envisaged the new college as an "English Leipzig". The college came into existence in 1893 and it became what is now the Royal Manchester College of Music.

As far as the orchestra was concerned, it was not until after Hallé's death that the nucleus of the Concerts Society came into being, and for three seasons, beginning in 1896, Mr. Behrens, Mr. James Forsyth, and Mr. Henry Simon, as "original guarantors", agreed to carry the concerts on, and to pay any net surplus up to £500 in each season to Hallé's executors. About £1,800 had been paid over to the executors at the end of this period.

In 1898 the Hallé Concerts Society was formed with E. J. Broadfield (Chairman), Gustav Behrens, Dr. Brodsky (Principal of the College of Music), James Forsyth, and James Aikman Forsyth (secretary) on the committee.

No permanent conductor had been appointed so long as the future of the concerts had remained obscure, but in October 1898, Gustav Behrens, Dr. Brodsky, and one or two others, went to London to meet Hans Richter, and they persuaded him to accept the post. In the meantime there had been several guest conductors, among them Sir Arthur Sullivan, Stanford, Barnby, Mackenzie, Brodsky, and Henschel. For the three years before Richter arrived, in October 1899, to assume control, Frederick Cowen was sole conductor.

Richter was then probably the world's leading conductor and during the twelve years he stayed in Manchester he raised the orchestra higher in the esteem of the critical musical world than it had ever stood, even in Hallé time. The reason had a good deal to do with Richter's own prestige. Hallé had too many interests, as soloist at his own concerts, as organizer and promoter, as well as conductor, to have been considered a conductor of the first-rank. But he had built the foundations in forty years of strenuous music-making of

127

the whole of the musical structure of the North. He had created a climate in which Richter could find full play for his autocratic genius. And it was due to this, and to the efforts of Gustav Behrens and his friends, that Richter was able to devote himself entirely to the technical perfection of the orchestra and to educating the public musically.

In the words of Mr. Russell, he " enhanced the solid classical tradition which Hallé had instituted, and which is still the backbone of Manchester's musical culture ". Apart from that it must be remembered in Richter's favour that he introduced Elgar's work to Manchester, indeed, almost forced Elgar on Manchester.

He retired, according to Mr. Behrens, because of failing health, but Mr. Russell states: " There was rather more to it than that. A small but brilliant and vociferous band of modernists arose in the city and Richter was attacked for failing to fall in with their views. As a young man I remember being present at a concert when a section of the audience revolted and showed its disapproval of the conductor by the singular method of applauding Zimbalist, the soloist. I can still picture Richter's broad and impassive back as he stood on the rostrum, silently adamant, and Zimbalist's repeated ' curtains ' and embarrassed bows as the conductor refused to make any acknowledgement. Richter won that round, and Samuel Langford made a discreet reference to the ' shindy ' in the Manchester Guardian the next day. But the modernists had their way in the end, and Richter had to go."

Michael Ballin was the Hallé's next conductor, but as a German, he was obliged to resign when the Kaiser's war broke out in 1914. Ballin brought Bruckner's and Mahler's symphonies to Manchester, as well as Stravinsky's music.

It was during the Kaiser's war that Sir Thomas Beecham performed not the least of his many services to the Hallé Orchestra in stepping into the breach. He continued to carry the orchestra along until Hamilton Harty was appointed permanent conductor in 1920. Harty, knighted later, remained until 1933, when he resigned.

Harty found the orchestra in need of rebuilding and carried this task out with his usual energy. According to Mr. Russell, he "made many friends and a few opponents to whom his temperament did not appeal". Mr. Russell adds: "Some time ago I wrote of Harty that ' his work had a slice of sentiment which sometimes slowed down the adagios, and a streak of devilment that occasionally whipped up the scherzos and finales, but lent to picturesque music a strangely graphic power '. I see no reason to alter that view."

From 1933 onwards the orchestra suffered inevitably from the absence of continuity in its musical direction. The players were apt to be confused by the different methods of each conductor, just as the public, or those among them who were discerning enough, were apt to be equally confused by the variety of interpretations of the same works.

Mr. Russell's little book, from which we have quoted so liberally here, was published in 1938. He asks: "And the orchestra, what is it like to-day? How does it compare with that of Sir Charles Hallé. We have the authority of a former leader to guide us. Willy Hess, who for some years was leader of the Hallé, came back to Manchester for a season three or four years ago as guest-professor at the Royal Manchester College of Music. He had nothing but a supreme admiration for the present orchestra, and remarked that in Sir Charles Hallé's day there was nothing of this brilliance and verve, the dash, the ensemble, the technique! Certain it is that visiting conductors have paid the highest tributes to the orchestra. Last year Weingartner said that he had expected to find the band good, but was very agreeably surprised at its all-round excellence. . . ."

A year after Mr. Russell wrote that another world war had

broken out and the Hallé had entered another critical period in its history. The war, however, opened up new possibilities which compensated for the uncertainty of things. Chief among these was the unexpectedly great demand for orchestral music which spread among war-workers and the armed forces. This in time led to the giving of countless concerts by the orchestra all over the North in war-factories, public halls and even cathedrals, concerts sponsored by C.E.M.A. and E.N.S.A. Beecham in these days was in America and it fell to Sargent, during the first two or three years of the war, to bear the brunt of conducting the Hallé concerts in Manchester, in Sheffield, and in other cities.

Then it was that Liverpool formed its own full-time orchestra, partly from the disbanded B.B.C. Salon orchestra, and Sargent was appointed its permanent conductor. This deprived the Hallé of his undivided services and created the situation in which the Hallé Committee were obliged to apply a drastic—and permanent—solution. The fortunes of the society had, indeed, reached the most serious crisis in its history. Half measures and temporizing would have been fatal at that juncture, but the Hallé Committee were helped to a decision by the fact that just at that moment, early in 1943, John Barbirolli had become available and was eager to return to his native country.

The man behind the society's decision to "burn its boats", to reconstruct the orchestra, and to invite Barbirolli to become permanent conductor, was Philip Godlee. Godlee is an amateur musician—he plays the viola—and the head of a Manchester firm of cotton maunfacturers. He is also chairman of the society which runs the thirty-one-year-old Manchester Tuesday Midday Concerts—started in 1916 as " Music in Wartime "—and of the British Federation of Music Festivals.

The son of a solicitor and born in Birmingham in

1890, he was educated at Marlborough where, he told the present writer, he "neglected his classical studies for music", which was then regarded as a slightly disreputable way of wasting time. He played the violin and (with the school band) the euphonium, and was sergeant bugler in the O.T.C. He went to Manchester to "seek his fortune" in 1914, but got into the army and was partly disabled by wounds in 1916. "Since 1918", he says, "I have indulged a passion for chamber music and changed from the violin to the viola, for which I have no regrets. I have four children—so as to have a family string quartet! "

Godlee is one of those men who so often shoot to the top in a crisis—they shoot to the top because of their gifts of vision and imagination.

The Hallé might easily have jogged along as it was doing under guest conductors and sharing its players' time and service with the B.B.C. But it would have been a sort of masquerade. There might even have been a strong temptation, with the war still on, to leave things as they were. But Godlee resisted it. The moment had come for a galvanizing impulse. War or no war the attempt had to be made to recover the orchestra's departed glory, or see it sink for good to the level of something purely provincial and second rate. As chairman of the committee and trustee of the orchestra's great tradition, Godlee realized that nothing short of a master-stroke could meet the situation.

And so a master-stroke it was. Not only was it decided to reconstruct the orchestra, under Barbirolli, but it was also proposed that the new Hallé should tour the country and give more than two hundred concerts every year. This was, in fact, a logical necessity involved in the process of placing all the members of the orchestra on yearly contracts and keeping them fully employed all the year round. The same necessity likewise obliged the new Liverpool Philharmonic to give most of its concerts outside its home city. In effect, the Hallé was to become a national orchestra in a geographical sense as well as by virtue of its prestige and history, as it had been for many years already. And it was when he learned of this that Barbirolli had said: " I face the hardest task of my career ".

For a long time the Hallé Society had only a small office on the premises of Forsyth's, the music shop in Deansgate, Manchester. Its staff consisted of a secretary and a typist. It was now necessary to take a suite of offices in one of Manchester's city squares, facing the great Central Library and the Midland Hotel. A general manager, Mr. T. E. Bean, was appointed, with an administrative staff that soon began to find the new offices too small.

To send the Hallé on tour for months on end meant a colossal amount of office work and planning. And in all this the society has been fortunate in Mr. Bean, a man of infinite resource, a tireless enthusiast. Instead of spending about £5,000 a year, the society cheerfully faced the prospect of an expenses sheet of something like £70,000. And at that time no financial help whatever was forthcoming from the city. The society have since succeeded in obtaining a grant from the Manchester Corporation, which, originally £2,500, now amounts to £15,000.

Of this, £6,000 is for fourteen children's concerts and the remaining £9,000 takes the form of a guarantee against loss, while the City Council has the right to have three representatives on the committee of the Hallé Concerts Society. But early in 1943 all this could not be envisaged, and according to the society's reconstruction scheme, Manchester itself was to hear no more than twenty-five per cent of the total number of concerts.

The only hall available in the city for the mid-week subscription concerts was the Albert Hall, belonging to a religious body, and opposite to the ruins of the old Free Trade Hall in Peter Street. The hall holds 1,750 people, and it was decided to duplicate each mid-week programme on successive nights, so that 3,500 of the regular subscribers might hear it.

In addition, a series of Sunday afternoon concerts was arranged for the King's Hall, in the famous Belle Vue Pleasure Gardens. Here it was possible to accommodate between 5,000 and 6,000 people. This meant that up to 9,000 would be able to hear the orchestra each week in Manchester during a season lasting from October until the following Spring. During the remaining months of the year except July, when the members of the orchestra had their annual holiday, the orchestra was to be on tour throughout England and Scotland, giving an average of five concerts a week in the course of a year.

The Hallé had always, even in Hallé's time, been in the habit of visiting several other cities and towns, as well as London, during a six-months' season. Sheffield's Philharmonic Society had for some years engaged the orchestra for their regular weekly concerts. And there had been no other orchestra available for the performances given by the great Yorkshire choirs controlled by the late Sir Henry Coward and his successors. Hanley, in the Potteries, could always be counted upon for a successful Hallé concert. For nearly half a century the Potteries has been a " hotbed of music " and even London impresarios have invariably included it in their " celebrity concert circuit " and have been well rewarded.

The taste had originally grown out of the Hallé's visits and it spread until music became as much a part of the life of the Potteries as its traditional industry.

The loyalty of the northern cities and towns could safely be counted upon in planning the new and greatly extended itineries of the reconstructed orchestra. But scores of other towns which had seldom or never heard the orchestra had to be added to the list. Moreover, at the time that all this bold planning was being done by Godlee and his committee, although the society had engaged Barbirolli, there was yet only the nucleus of an orchestra for him to conduct, and it would be months before one would be in existence and trained sufficiently to make its bow before the public. But the planning had to go on and be near completion by the time Barbirolli reached England in the early summer of 1943.

There were many elements of risk. For one thing the war still had its course to run, although a victorious end was already in sight. For another, the war-time boom in orchestral music might not last. Then again, there was the problem of persuading the local concert societies to agree to a financial arrangement by which the orchestra would be guaranteed its full fee. This meant in many cases that the local societies had to seek some form of guarantee against loss among their own members or from the civic authorities.

There proved to be no difficulty in this arrangement, and the city of Sheffield eventually showed a fine spirit by making the Philharmonic Society a grant of £5,000 a year, which was, in effect, a grant to enable them to engage the Hallé Orchestra for the whole season. Other cities acted in the same way, although not always on the same scale. In a sense, this readiness to provide financial support was a tribute to the high standing of the Hallé Orchestra wherever concerts were arranged.

The courage of Godlee and his associates was rewarded, as courage is always rewarded, by the making of friends, and by creating new loyalties. As far as the other element of risk—the possible transcience of the war-time music boom—was concerned, a bold policy again could eliminate it. In the event the risk has proved negligible, and no risk at all. If anything, in the years following the end of the war the public appetite for orchestral music, far from flagging, has seemed almost inexhaustible. And this is the outstanding fact of music in our time.

At all events, the Hallé planners found that all the cities and towns were ready to welcome the orchestra as soon as, and as often as, it cared to visit them.

On their journey back to England Mr. and Mrs. Barbirolli had a lucky escape, although it involved tragedy for others. At Lisbon they accepted seats in a plane leaving for London in two days' time instead of going by the one for which they had booked. The plane they were to have travelled in was shot down by the Germans and all the passengers perished, among them Leslie Howard, the film star.

On arriving in Manchester, the Barbirollis were the guests of Mr. Godlee at his Alderley Edge home, and then moved into their flat at Rusholme.

Soon Barbirolli had his programmes to think of, programmes not only for the society's subscription concerts and the more popular concerts at Belle Vue, but also for those to be given to Forces audiences and war-workers. He entered upon this task, and upon the business of training, almost from scratch, his new orchestra with a vitality and enthusiasm which he had not known in those last months in America. It must have seemed a gracious gesture of Providence to him that now, after longing to come back home to play some part in the war in his native country, he was at last given the chance to do it in the way best suited to his gifts.

Now he had the deep satisfaction of knowing that while following his professional career and doing great work in it, he could at the same time bring some beauty and enjoyment, some great inspiration, it may-be, into the daily lives of those in the military and industrial front line. He was never able to feel that way in America, where he was virtually a stranger in a foreign land. His patriotism was always a sensitive thing. When it was frustrated he was unhappy, and even his professional triumphs in America could not make him feel different.

During the summer of 1943, after his return home, he might claim to be a happy man, in spite of the heavy task before him. Indeed, it was more than probable that the feeling of being " home " again with his wife eased that task considerably. He talked freely to the Press about everything—that is, about everything but his six years of success in America. Apart from brief cables appearing in our own newspapers, the public over here had no way of knowing the full story of how the young unknown Englishman had shed new lustre over America's greatest orchestra and had not suffered in comparisons with Toscanini himself. Yet for most people the fact that Barbirolli had held that high post for six years was in itself sufficient.

It is certain that he came back " stiff with prestige ", a far bigger man, in every sense, than he was when he set out for New York in 1936. Yet was he at heart the same man, modest, entirely free from arrogance, warm-blooded and vital, without any illusions about either himself or his job. Nor could he have found a moment more suitable for his return, or a more fitting role in which to establish himself in Britain's musical life than as conductor of a reconstructed Hallé Orchestra. The possibilities were limited only by the number and quality of the orchestral players available and financial resources.

When it came to fixing the size of the orchestra, Barbirolli realized that he must be content for the time being with one somewhat below full strength. The main reason for this was

that in most of the halls in which the orchestra would have
to play there would not be room for one of a hundred or
even of ninety players. Even so, the orchestra has never
consisted of fewer than seventy-two players. It now stands
at eighty and, when the Free Trade Hall in Manchester is
once more available, it will be brought up to full strength
in accordance with the plans of the society. In the meantime, a body of eighty and even seventy players in the hands
of a man like Barbirolli can—and does—produce a quality
of tone which compares favourably with that produced by
larger orchestras. But whatever the size of the new orchestra
Barbirolli's task in the beginning was formidable enough.
He had always been endowed with boundless energy. He
needed it now and at once began to prove that he could
outstay anybody around him. You cannot imagine this
dynamic man, " crackling with energy ", as has been said
of him, in repose. His body may relax, but never his mind.
It is in this superabundance of physical and mental energy,
standing out in such vivid contrast to the " unassuming "
air of the outward man that has marked him off from the rest.
It was, too, the crucible in which the new Hallé was to be
forged. The impact of all this energy and of his unusually
keen intelligence on his players was to produce before a
year was out results for which astonishing would not be too
strong a word. It was to make the few old Hallé players
who had remained, especially Charles Collier, feel that in
their new conductor was a force not less remarkable than
the greatest of those who had gone before. These are not
superlatives, but facts, and with a man like Barbirolli facts
always speak louder than superlatives.

CHAPTER XIII

BARBIROLLI'S " MIRACLE "

THE Hallé Concerts Society, having seen the last of those of the old orchestra who had gone over to the B.B.C., advertised for players, so that there would be as many as possible for Barbirolli to choose from when, as he proposed, he was ready to give auditions in London and Manchester. There was a surprisingly good response. Barbirolli took up his post on June 1, 1943. The orchestra had to be made up to seventy players in the space of barely a month and to be ready for the opening concert of the Bradford festival week on July 5th. This was the first stage of Barbirolli's " miracle ", of which people afterwards spoke.

In the London auditions Barbirolli heard players from the Royal Academy and Royal College of Music, and up north he made several " finds " at the Royal Manchester College of Music.

But for many of the players he had to go outside the schools. Some had never played in a symphony orchestra before, and in selecting his players Barbirolli placed technique and musicianship before orchestral experience because, as he said, " It is better to have musicians who play well, without orchestral experience, than players with orchestral experience who do not play so well."

" These auditions were heartbreaking," he said, " but it was the only way. I gave the new players some stiff test pieces, but they mastered them all." For rehearsals the society took over a disused school at the back of Manchester's Central Station, one of the ugliest and dirtiest buildings in all Manchester, and in one of the city's ugliest back streets, Hewitt Street. But if the surroundings were drab and uninspiring, what went on high up on the top floor of the old school made up for everything.

Barbirolli concentrated on the weaker parts of the orchestra, which contained the players who were strangers to symphonic music. But as these players' musical skill and intelligence were in inverse ratio to their experience, they were eager pupils. He found that his young, inexperienced players more than made up in enthusiasm what they lacked in experience. In a little while they could even surprise their seasoned and cosmopolitan conductor. As he said later, he " could not have believed it possible " for these young players to rise so quickly to the highest standards of performance. In great part this had been due to his own hard work and training, but it showed him that he had chosen well and surely.

" Rehearsals began at 9.30 in the mornings—three hours for strings, three for brass and wood-wind, and three all together " says Mr. Godlee. " And in that week of rehearsals, J. B. did nine hours a day conducting, and spent most of the night bowing parts." That must have been one of the most hectic weeks in British orchestral history.

The day before rehearsals began, on June 27th, the old Hallé gave its farewell concert as an orchestra at Stretford, in aid of the memorial fund to Leslie Heward, Boult's successor with the City of Birmingham Orchestra. Sargent conducted, and Barbirolli sat in the audience. Then the old orchestra dispersed and the new came into being.

The final rehearsal was held in Houldsworth Hall, Deansgate, Manchester, before a number of critics and others. The *Yorkshire Post* music critic was there and wrote: " There can be no doubt that a miracle has been achieved with the newly-formed orchestra. . . . The result [of the Houldsworth Hall concert] was simply to dispel any questionings about the orchestra's quality which one might have had in view of the present difficulty of finding orchestral players. . . . Barbirolli's methods exemplify the truth about genius being an infinite capacity for taking pains. Each one of countless repetitions has its own exciting possibility, that it might produce his approving shout of ' That's it! ' . . . The conducting of Barbirolli made the experience a revelation."

Before the opening concert at Bradford a little matter of musical politics had to be settled. The Bradford Concert Society's Committee had arranged, out of seven concerts, for no fewer than five piano concertos. Barbirolli refused to conduct such performances. " I have not come all the way from America," he said—a little indignantly—" to accompany guest artists." The committee went over in a body to Manchester to discuss the matter with him and to plead for their concertos. But Barbirolli would not budge. The utmost concession he would make was one concerto and no more.

And one concerto it was, after the committee had declared in a public statement issued after the meeting in Manchester: " Mr. Barbirolli's attitude towards the appearance of such artists at Hallé Concerts affects all the centres in which the orchestra will play during its tour of the country, but that aspect of the matter was not raised by the deputation."

When this question had been amicably settled, all was ready for the new Hallé's début at the Princes Theatre, Bradford. It was all too certain that the first thing that would occur to the older generation among the audiences, at least in Manchester itself, and to the music critics at large, would be to judge the new orchestra by the standards of the old, and of the old, not in its decline, but in its heyday.

Thus there was much at stake, and not least, perhaps,

Barbirolli's own reputation. The critics, at any rate, knowing more about the inside of the situation than the public, were prepared to make full allowance for the fact that this " phoenix " orchestra bearing the name of the Hallé could not have been expected, even under the hands of such a master as Barbirolli, to rise to its full stature until it had been passed through the ordeal of public performance. At the most they expected a competent first performance, with characteristic Barbirolli flashes of brilliance here and there. Some might have looked forward to nothing more than a masterly display of conducting against a background of orchestral playing. From this point of view Barbirolli would be present as a solo performer with the orchestra for accompaniment.

The general musical public did not know what was in store for them. All they knew was that they were going to hear an orchestra with a much-honoured and famous name, conducted by a man of whom they had read much in the newspapers from time to time and whose personality had somehow made itself felt among them without their ever having come in contact with him. They had seen the name, " John Barbirolli " in big letters on the posters around the town, and vaguely this name meant something. Most of them probably had not the smallest notion of the upheaval which had all but extinguished an orchestra, or, if they had, did not appreciate its significance. To musical people in the North, there would always be a Hallé, just as there would always be an England.

The choice of Bradford, busy centre of the woollen industry, for the orchestra's début was not altogether a question of tactics, or of " trying it on the dog ", but chiefly of seasonal arrangements. Those Bradford people who, like Lord Calverley in a House of Lords debate, claim that it was Bradford that " gave the Hallé Orchestra to the country ", because some of their forebears had helped Hallé to maintain his original band, might have taken the " première " as an acknowledgement of this early contribution. The main reason was that the season in Manchester was not due to open until later. But Barbirolli may, all the same, have welcomed the opportunity of trying out the orchestra somewhere outside Manchester, so that it could shed some of its immaturity. And yet Bradford, one of the most musical of cities, could be as fastidious and exacting as any community in the country.

In any case, as it was known to be the orchestra's first performance, critics from all over the country came to bear down on it. No matter where it took place, it would have aroused the same wide interest which it, in fact, did.

Thus around this first concert in Bradford there was a tense feeling of expectancy. The Princes Theatre was packed that night, and the rest of the week, justifying Barbirolli's contention that there will always be a good audience for a purely orchestral programme. At the first concert, the works played included the *Meistersingers* overture, Delius's *Song of Summer*, and the Brahms's Second Symphony.

Of this concert, Granville Hill wrote in the *Manchester Guardian*: " The rehearsals in Manchester . . . were of the most exacting and comprehensive nature, so this orchestra of seventy members has already started in downright earnest towards its goal of a firmly welded yet pliable ensemble." He added: " Several of the women in the band, of whom two play the horn and one the double-bass, are so young that they cannot have had much orchestral experience and their adaptability to present conditions has yet to be proved, as also their fitness for the strenuous life with a travelling company." He went on: " That these youthful members are clever executants was shown unmistakably in last night's concert. They had no easy time. Mr. Barbirolli conducted with the utmost intensity of style and called for a similarly concentrated expression from the players. His vitality was at once apparent in the graphic readings of the *Meistersinger* overture."

Hill ended his notice by saying: " Such faults as we have mentioned can, of course, be quickly overcome, and in a little while the new Hallé ensemble should show a splendid unity and eloquence." This may not have been wild praise, but it was, perhaps, the most that could have been expected for an orchestra collected together in four short weeks, which had had only a week's rehearsal. As the week went on the new orchestra was further tested and Barbirolli was able to see how the weak spots stood revealed in public performance. During the week it was reported that among the sheaves of telegrams wishing Barbirolli success were some from old members of the British National Opera Company. On one of the days fell the fourth anniversary of Barbirolli's marriage to Evelyn Rothwell.

The *Manchester Guardian* reported that: " Mr. John Barbirolli, interviewed last night at Bradford, said he was highly pleased with the artistic and business success of the new Hallé's concerts, which are nearing their close in the city. . . . Hundreds of people have been turned away and there have been gallery queues as early as four o'clock in the afternoon—two and a half hours before the concerts begin. . . . Mr. Barbirolli declared he was fully satisfied with the tone, quality, and ensemble of the players."

A Yorkshire newspaper wrote, the day after the concert in which the only piano concerto—with Clifford Curzon— was played: " ' Why is it so crowded to-night? ' was the question somebody put just before the opening of the Hallé concert at the Bradford Princes Theatre last night. Pointing to the programme somebody else commented: ' Grieg '.

Well, it may have been Grieg's piano concerto that helped to fill the theatre. When the concerto ended, having been adorned by masterly solo work by Clifford Curzon, there was a vociferous demonstration—apparently intended for John Barbirolli's attention in view of his having cut out all the other concertos originally proposed. But if this was so, the rest of the concert seemed to indicate a change of heart on the part of, at any rate, a section of the audience. So adroitly did Mr. Barbirolli push forward his claim for the orchestra to be heard alone that the outburst of cheering at the end of the concert far eclipsed the previous one in fervour. . . . It was clear that Mr. Barbirolli had taken great pains to make sure that the orchestra would give a performance much above the average. His personality was written all over it; he whipped his forces into a frenzy of excitement in the Venusberg music and he got first-class co-operation from everybody in bringing off a majestic final statement of the ' Pilgrim ' theme."

And the *News Chronicle* reported that in response to an ovation, Barbirolli had said: " This is in a way an occasion. I have been entrusted with a very great mission—that the name and fame of this great orchestra shall not, under my guidance, achieve less honour in the future than it has done in the past." Once more Barbirolli had displayed his gift for saying the right word.

After that memorable first week in Bradford the orchestra returned to Manchester for further intensive rehearsal, in readiness for the next series of concerts in Scotland. But before he left Bradford, Barbirolli expressed some interesting views on the week's experience to the *Yorkshire Observer*. The journalist, remarking that a third of the orchestra were women, asked if the women " produced less tone " than the men. Barbirolli replied: " That is all nonsense. Production of tone, whether on wind or string instruments, is not a

IN VIENNA IN 1947

WITH JOSEF KRIPS

REFLECTIONS OUTSIDE BEETHOVEN'S HOUSE
IN VIENNA

question of physical strength, it is a personal gift. Just as you come across small men with big voices, so you come across musicians of slender physique who can produce tremendous tone. Don't forget that you were hearing the orchestra this week on a theatre stage. You got half the tone they really have. In the concert hall they will be as powerful as a 100 per cent male orchestra. Don't forget that the B.B.C. Orchestra, the first English orchestra that Toscanini conducted, was 40 per cent women. What matters is not volume of tone, but its quality."

By such remarks Barbirolli was always giving some insight into the ideas and methods he brought to bear in training an orchestra. Quality rather than quantity. The *Yorkshire Post* summed up: "Last week's Hallé Concerts at Bradford . . . provided gratifying evidence in support of arguments which have been increasingly disregarded in recent years. They showed that a piano concerto is not a condition precedent to success in the building of a concert programme, and they proved also that granted an adequate number of rehearsals, the brilliance and vitality in an ensemble mainly composed of young players can be turned to satisfactory account in the first week of its existence. . . . Not least welcome has been the realization that in Mr. Barbirolli we have one of the greatest conductors of the day."

To the *Yorkshire Observer*, in the interview already quoted, Barbirolli offered an explanation of his attitude towards concertos. "I have been misunderstood about concertos," he said. "All that I am against is their abuse. Concertos are among the world's best music and they will play their due part in Hallé concert schemes." Barbirolli's sudden stand for the rights of the orchestra, and of purely orchestral music, even in the midst of war-time cares, startled many people who had accepted without question the "concerto" fetish. In the end they felt he was right. He may have seemed, too, a little ahead of his time. But as against the concerto he had reason on his side. Most of the stock concerto classics are dreadfully overworked, and need a long rest.

And so back to Manchester, to scheme for a series of concerts at Edinburgh—the orchestra's next venture. Transport was not the least among the Society's problems. Rail travel during the war years was extremely uncomfortable and uncertain, and to transport seventy players, with their instruments and luggage and precious music scores, up and down the country was to become a constant headache to the Society's management. It was also, combined with rehearsals on reaching each town, to tax the strength of the members of the orchestra and of the conductor almost beyond endurance. But musicians seem to be tough, and although a few of the Hallé players fell out, most of them got through little the worse for their strenuous travelling, which included a tour near the fighting line in Belgium and Holland during the last winter of the war, when as background for their music they would sometimes have gunfire and bomb explosions in the distance. Among the Hallé players who never missed a journey, or even a trip to the war-front, was Charles Collier, the harpist, although he was over seventy. And Collier, on these travels, would, when he felt inclined, talk to the new members of the orchestra about Richter as familiarly as he could talk about Barbirolli.

CHAPTER XIV

THE HALLÉ ON TOUR

AFTER the opening concert at Bradford and a return to Manchester for intensive rehearsal, the Hallé Orchestra and Barbirolli visited first Edinburgh and then Glasgow, to give a week of concerts in each city. Both cities remembered the time when Barbirolli had put new life into the Scottish Orchestra, and gave him and his reconstituted Hallé a big welcome.

The Usher Hall in Edinburgh, and the St. Andrew's Hall in Glasgow, were sold out for memorable programmes which included works by Schubert, Brahms, Delius; and the Dvořák " New World " Symphony—programmes wisely chosen to set off all the brilliant tone of the new Hallé, without unduly taxing its technical resources.

The visits proved an outstanding experience, both to the music-lovers of the two cities and for the orchestra players. Since then the two weeks of concerts, one in each city, have become an annual event, and year by year Edinburgh and Glasgow have been able to observe stages by which the Hallé has become, in the words of a London critic, " Britain's premier orchestra ".

Before the orchestra made its début in the home city of Manchester, on August 15, 1943, other cities and towns were visited, including Newcastle, Harrogate, Leeds, Halifax, and Wolverhampton.

One or two of these cities were seeing Barbirolli for the first time, as well as the orchestra. In a two-column article

147

on the "rebirth of the Hallé", the *Yorkshire Post* music editor wrote of it: "During the last two months an event of epoch-making importance has occurred in the world of music". And of Barbirolli: "What kind of importance attaches to the presence of this conductor in this country? This I think and nothing less—that it is on a par with the coming to England last century of Sir Charles Hallé and Richter themselves. We are so accustomed to sending our men of genius out of the country in order that another nation may discover the greatness we cannot have fully appreciated that when the process goes full circle, and the genius returns to give us the benefit of his new experience, we are hard put to it to understand the greatness of the gesture. The gesture on this occasion amounts to this, that Barbirolli has deliberately chosen to leave the scene of the greatest triumph and highest honour music has to bestow—the conductorship in succession to Toscanini of the New York Philharmonic Symphony Orchestra—to devote his genius to the training of an orchestra (whose business it is to give us the real sound of real music) with all the hazards and uncertainty inseparable from such a venture in war-time. Genius he certainly has. . . . Years after Barbirolli had taken over Toscanini returned as guest conductor to the New York orchestra and said that it was every bit as great as when he left it. . . . But reassurances of that kind are no longer necessary when many have heard Barbirolli conduct. . . . On page after page, for example, in the Brahms Symphony one could hear the Hallé Orchestra producing effects, finished touches, that one had never imagined could be there. For the string section alone every score they play has already been marked as to bowing by a man whose knowledge of string playing is a part of his genius. This is not simply a matter of making the movement of bows identical. There is a world of difference in tone between an up-bow and a down-bow, and

Barbirolli seems to know every variety of tone that can be produced and exactly which to choose."

The orchestra's opening concert in Manchester took place in the King's Hall, Belle Vue, before 6,000 people. " At last " wrote Granville Hill, the *Manchester Guardian* critic, " after having achieved glowing success on tour, the newly formed Hallé Orchestra has been heard for the first time in its home town, and yesterday, a crowd, mighty in size and enthusiasm, listened for a couple of hours to splendid playing. . . . A good deal of the orchestral playing was indeed finer than any we have heard in Manchester for many years."

The programme consisted of *The Mastersingers* overture, Debussy's prelude *L'Après midi d'un Faun*, Elgar's *Enigma Variations*, and Tchaikovsky's Fifth Symphony, a programme which needs only to be stated to understand how the playing of it moved every one of the 6,000 present.

Granville Hill went on: ". . . the beauty and brilliancy of the playing proved that the period during which the orchestra might claim indulgence because its members have not been playing together long enough will be passed very much sooner than could have been expected. . . . Throughout each work Mr. Barbirolli conducted superbly, his qualities of leadership impressing in equal degree players and audience."

The great audience also exhibited a mass of enthusiasm seldom before encountered. It was much the same when Barbirolli and the orchestra gave their first concert in Sheffield. There, before the concert, there had been a civic reception. Later, at the concert, the deputy Lord Mayor, not to be outdone in praise, referred to Barbirolli as " World Conductor No. 1 ". This brought a letter in the *Sheffield Telegraph* next day from a reader signing himself " Platform Ticket ", which stated: " Sir,—At last Friday's Philharmonic Concert the deputy Lord Mayor referred to Mr.

Barbirolli as ' World Conductor No. 1 '. Does he not realize
that the value of a truly great conductor is not assessable. To
place Barbirolli, No. 1, Toscanini, No. 2, etc., would be really
too ridiculous. Let us say that Mr. Barbirolli is one of
the world's great conductors (we can judge that by the
response he gets and the results he obtains) and just leave it
at that! "

Others were not shy in coming forward to remind newspaper readers of the great services to the Hallé at difficult
times by Beecham, Sargent, and others—voices that were
useful and necessary in preserving a sense of proportion.

The concert at Sheffield began a weekly series to be given
by the Hallé during that season and every season since. Still
the regular season had not begun in Manchester, and in the
meantime, concerts were given in suburbs like Stretford and
Didsbury. Then followed ENSA concerts for war workers
all over the North. A writer in the *Manchester Evening
News* said about the visit to Wigan: " John Barbirolli, with
his wide range of knowledge of audience psychology, had to
go to Wigan, conducting the first sixpenny ENSA factory
concert, to get the surprise of his career. This was his
audience's wild applause to the long-shot of the programme
—Debussy's *L'Après midi d'un Faun.* That was their
favourite, and not the more popular *Mastersingers* overture
or the *Eine Kleine Nachmusik.* Flinging down his baton in
his dressing-room when it was all over, he said to Laurance
Turner, the leader of the orchestra: " I can't get over it . . .
the way they reacted to the *Après midi,* which was hissed
when it was first heard in Paris. . . . I see the age of miracles
is not yet past."

Young people, especially girls, said this writer, pre-
dominated in the audience and, " like their fellow-workers,
listened with rapt attention ". The general comment was
" a reet good do ", among workers who had never been to a

symphony concert before. Barbirolli said: " What a marvellous audience! How did they know not to applaud
between the movements of the symphony? This is the sort
of thing you often get even at ' fashionable ' concerts. Here
—it was grand. I felt the audience was with me all the
time."

What happened at this workers' concert was repeated,
with local variations, at all of them.

On October 10th, Barbirolli made his first appearance in
London since his return from America, beginning the
one-hundred-and-thirty-second season of the Royal Philharmonic Society, the oldest musical society in the world, at the
Albert Hall, this time with the London Philharmonic
Orchestra. *The Times* critic wrote that it was " notable for
the choice of programme and the beauty of the orchestral
playing. The credit for both goes to the conductor, Mr.
John Barbirolli ".

The critic went on: " Mr. Barbirolli's method is to treat
the music he plays as a fluent, plastic surface on which
orchestral detail can be inscribed with great delicacy. . . . He
galvanizes his orchestra with animation and insists on nuance
of tone. . . ."

Of the performance of the Mozart C major Symphony
(No. 34), the critic said: " Beecham used to give it a whip-
chord effect. Mr. Barbirolli's performance was crisp enough,
but its baroque curves were softer, and he made the slow
movement a thing of tenderness." In Stravinsky's *Firebird*
suite there was " the outstanding performance in an afternoon of fine playing . . . such a *pianissimo* from the strings
is rare indeed nowadays. Mr. Barbirolli evoked not only
the Firebird's magic, but almost the visual reality of the
ballet ".

During a visit of the Hallé Orchestra to Nottingham in
November, Barbirolli met Serjeant John Woolford, of the

U.S. Army, who had been his personal secretary in New York. This was one of many similar meetings in this country with friends he had made in New York.

In Manchester, the regular season had begun with mid-week concerts at the Albert Hall and Sunday concerts before audiences of 6,000 at Belle Vue. The critics, week by week, noted some new improvement, some old weakness removed. The orchestra was getting into its stride. In January Barbirolli took it to Birmingham. "The new Hallé Orchestra", wrote one critic there, "gave its first Birmingham concert in the Town Hall last night and worthily carried on a great tradition. It has been reconstituted and revitalized under John Barbirolli, who returned from America to undertake this important work. His success has been remarkable. In the main, the orchestra consists of young players who possess not only surprising skill but a tremendous enthusiasm. In short, they are musicians. True to tradition, the glory of the orchestra is its strings. Their tone, no less than their immaculate technique, stamp them immediately as first-rate."

The critic recalled the old Hallé leader, the late Arthur Catterall, and said he "would not have been ashamed of the new players." He adds: "The measure of the orchestra's success is the faithfulness with which it responds to its conductor's wish and mood."

In the same month, Granville Hill wrote, in the *Manchester Guardian*, of a concert in Manchester: "The playing throughout was exuberant and sure proof of the Hallé Orchestra's advance to virtuosity since Mr. John Barbirolli has been in command was the fact that the great speed at which the quick movements were taken involved no loss of point or colour."

Towards the end of January 1944, Barbirolli was again in London, conducting the London Philharmonic Orchestra in the Royal Philharmonic Society's concert at the Albert Hall. "The concert . . ." wrote Ralph Hill in the *Sunday Times*, " was a model of programme building. Furthermore, on the rostrum was a conductor who is a fine musician, a sensitive artist, and a strong personality. Indeed, John Barbirolli stands alone in this country in possessing all these essential qualities. The effect on the London Philharmonic Orchestra was remarkable."

Musical Opinion said, of an item in the programme, Ravel's suite, *Ma Mère l'Oye*, that it " was given a very sensitive rendering—virtuoso orchestral playing at its best. Barbirolli excels in music of this type." *The Times* critic wrote: " A classical symphony rounded off a scheme which had offered in its earlier items opportunity for orchestral virtuosity which Mr. Barbirolli certainly knew how to produce ".

The same critic continued: " Virtuosity has its place in music elsewhere than in concertos, and the conductor's insistence on fine *pianissimo*, the utmost subtlety from the strings, and delicacy from the wind, produced highly polished performances of his own *Elizabethan Suite* and Ravel's *Ma Mère l'Oye*. . . . Ravel's fairy-tale picture-book had its enchantment enhanced by the calculated placing of orchestral effects."

Before the end of the month, Barbirolli and the Hallé, besides playing in Manchester, had visited Sheffield, Shrewsbury, and Blackpool. In Sheffield, about this time, in announcing that the city had given a grant of £1,000 to the Philharmonic Society there, Professor Shera, the chairman, said: " Under John Barbirolli the Hallé had achieved greater things than had been heard from it since the war started."

This was meant as no reflection on Dr. Malcolm Sargent, who had been conducting the orchestra in its regular Sheffield concert series. Sargent had not had an orchestra like the reconstituted Hallé.

In March 1944 Barbirolli was asked, for the purposes of an article by the present writer: " If you had to please yourself purely and simply, what would be your ideal concert programme? " Barbirolli replied: " If I approach the question from the angle of the last programme I should choose to conduct, say at a farewell concert, it would be: *Introduction and Allegro*, Elgar; Symphony No. 40 in G minor, Mozart; *La Mer*, Debussy; Symphony No. 4, Brahms."

As the months went by, Barbirolli was able to introduce more and more less familiar and new works, notably Vaughan Williams's Fifth Symphony.

The great popular concerts in the King's Hall, Manchester, were in full swing by April 1944, attracting audiences only equalled in size anywhere in Britain by those which filled the Royal Albert Hall, London.

And then, while the Hallé Orchestra was playing at Edinburgh in the following month, came a moment of great anxiety for the Hallé Society, and for the tens of thousands of followers of Barbirolli throughout the North of England. Barbirolli received the first of many offers to tempt him from the Hallé citadel and his vitally important work there. It came from London, from some sponsors of a grandiose scheme for employing the London Symphony Orchestra in a new series of operatic and other performances. Barbirolli described it as " a very tempting offer " and said he would " have to decide shortly ".

Barbirolli had not been impressed with the amount of support which the City of Manchester then proposed to give him in building up the orchestra and re-establishing it with its old tradition. It had, it is true, made a grant of £2,500 to the society, of which £1,000 was for children's concerts. This was a poor effort in the opinion of many people, compared with what other, and less wealthy, cities were doing. In this chilling atmosphere, Barbirolli must have asked himself whether it was worth while going on with the Hallé, and whether he would be justified, in the interests of music and of himself, in sacrificing other opportunities that were bound to present themselves from time to time. The offer meant a permanent conductorship in London with an orchestra which, after the Royal Philharmonic, was the oldest in the metropolis. It held out all the other advantages of living and working in an international centre.

These considerations weighed heavily with Barbirolli, and he was now faced with the most difficult decision of his life. He took a week or two to think it over. During that time he received many private appeals to stay in Manchester and continue the great work he had begun, and it was no doubt pointed out to him that probably nothing less than the continued existence of the Hallé depended on his decision.

These considerations weighed with him equally with the others, and in the end helped him to the point of rejecting the London offer. What finally decided him was the thought of what his departure would mean to the new audiences and the vast body of enthusiasts he had created in one short year. What it all amounted to was this: that it was largely the regard and enthusiasm for the Hallé Orchestra under Barbirolli displayed in other cities that had saved the Hallé a second time for Manchester.

Some time later, after receiving a tremendous ovation from a huge audience at Belle Vue, Manchester, Barbirolli turned to his manager and said: " One simply can't leave that! " So he has stayed, and taken his orchestra with him to new heights.

But there has been a compromise which has made it easier for him to turn down subsequent offers. That has been the arrangement by which he is released when necessary to conduct other orchestras, abroad as well as in London.

In September 1944 came Barbirolli's successful visit to Italy. He flew over to Naples and, with an Italian orchestra, gave a number of concerts for the Allied troops in the San Carlo Opera House.

" He found most comfortable quarters," it was reported, " but little symphony music. There was the music of one Beethoven Symphony (No. 5), but no Tchaikovsky except the ' 1812 ' Overture. There were no scores of Brahms. The Second Symphony had been available, but somebody had stolen it—' probably the German conductor,' said Mr. Barbirolli. In general there was almost nothing for a symphony orchestra to play except Italian opera."

Barbirolli flew to Rome and found enough music for two symphony concerts at Naples. " ' The orchestra,' said Mr. Barbirolli, ' was not first-rate,' " the report went on. " But it had some hard rehearsals. There was terrific enthusiasm from the orchestra and the audience, and the concert ended with everyone cheering wildly. Afterwards General Clark went round and thanked Mr. Barbirolli on behalf of the troops."

Concerts were held every night for a week after that, and the same works were repeated, " with rehearsals all day and every day " in Rome later.

In Rome Barbirolli had a better body of players in the Radio Orchestra, probably the best in Italy. He also conducted concerts at Taranto and Bari.

It was, incidentally, only the second time in his life that Barbirolli had visited the land of his fathers.

In Naples the musicians asked, " Why don't you stay here? " and told Barbirolli he was the " first great maestro to come to Italy for many years."

Writing to Bruno Zirato, assistant manager of the New

York Philharmonic Symphony Orchestra, he said he had made a discovery in the orchestra at Bari—a "magnificent violinist named Antonioni, the leader".

In November, back in England, Barbirolli was chosen to conduct at a great Anglo-American Thanksgiving concert in the Royal Albert Hall, London, before 8,000 people. "Apart from his eminence as a conductor," wrote the *Daily Telegraph*, "there's another reason which makes it especially appropriate that Barbirolli should be in charge of the musical programme." That reason was his association with the New York Orchestra; and the *Daily Telegraph* went on: "No other British conductor is in so good a position to interpret music by Americans, which naturally has so large a share in this typical American celebration. . . . At the climax Mr. Barbirolli had under his forceful baton not only the London Symphony Orchestra and the Alexander Choir, but the band of the Scots Guards and the Kneller Hall trumpeters."

The celebration was entitled, "To You, America". The programme was broadcast to the United States, and it was estimated that 30,000,000 people listened-in.

The London *Star* noted: "Music for Thanksgiving Day Festival at the Albert Hall was played by the London Symphony Orchestra under John Barbirolli—a conductor not properly appreciated here until he had made his mark in America."

CHAPTER XV

CONTINENTAL INTERLUDE

In December 1944, a little more than six months after D-Day, there took place an event unprecedented in the history of the Hallé—and in the history of war. For Barbirolli took his orchestra on a tour, lasting more than a fortnight, of the North-West Europe war zone. During one concert the entrance to the hall actually came under fire from enemy aircraft. It was the first time the Hallé had left these shores, and the first time since the " phoney " phase of early 1940 that a British orchestra had visited the Continent. Concerts were planned for Brussels, Antwerp, Ghent, Eindhoven, Lille, and Amiens, and one or two other towns. The tour was organized and sponsored by ENSA. It was mid-winter and very cold, but although it meant spending Christmas travelling and giving performances, instead of beside their own firesides, both Barbirolli and his orchestra eagerly seized the opportunity of going out with musical sustenance for the troops. And they were prepared to endure anything to make the tour a success. They were rewarded beyond their dreams by unforgettable experiences, not the least of which was the fervour and wild enthusiasm which marked every performance.

A number of concerts, in Sheffield and elsewhere, part of the regular season's programme, had to be cancelled so that the orchestra could undertake the tour. It was due to open at Brussels on December 20th, but the boat taking the orchestra to the Continent was delayed by fog and other bad weather conditions, and the first concert did not take place until two days later. Before leaving, all the members of the orchestra had to be inoculated, the first dose being administered in the train between Newcastle and Manchester. They gave their annual performance of the *Messiah* at Belle Vue on the Sunday, and next day packed their belongings and set off for Belgium. Mr. T. E. Bean, describing the first part of the tour in the *Manchester Guardian*, told how they had to spend two days in idleness at a transit camp in the South of England, to which they were taken in lorries without seats. " Eventually, on the third day, we found ourselves in the exciting darkness of a quayside, receiving an issue of iron rations." On the voyage over, the members of the orchestra gave on board the fog-ridden boat a concert which a *Manchester Guardian* correspondent described as " unlike any they have ever given, or are likely to give again ". The concert was in the form of a variety show. " Space," said the same correspondent, " was so cramped (there were many troops on board) that trombone players —to quote Mr. Barbirolli—were in danger of knocking the teeth out of some soldiers every time they played. Instead of symphony music they played songs for community singing. As the orchestral parts had been hurriedly written out on the backs of envelopes, and, in the absence of music stands, were being held in front of the players by Mr. Barbirolli and other volunteers, the effect was decidedly unsymphonic. Then, as a substitute for classical solos, certain members of the orchestra obliged with comic songs and startling instrumental *obbligatos*—arrayed in cloth caps, ' chokers ', and any other comic stage props they could lay hands on." As the fun developed, the versatility of the Hallé players seemed to impress their chief, who said: " I never knew I had such a completely crazy gang under my direction, and hiding their talent from me. I was wondering what was happening just at that moment in Brussels, where we should have been playing, and what our intended audience would say if they knew what we were actually doing just then. Puishnoff was a real brick to step into the breach" (the pianist had agreed to give a concert when the orchestra did not arrive in time).

The correspondent went on: " Not until after dark last evening "—his dispatch was dated, Brussels, December 22nd —" did this largest of all ENSA parties disembark. Hundreds of sandwiches and many gallons of tea were prepared for them and consumed while the instruments were unloaded. A convoy of motor coaches, troop-carrying vehicles, and three-ton trucks, in which the orchestra will be travelling from one place to another on tour, began the last stage of the journey [to Brussels], with the players singing at the top of their voices like real ' troupers '. They arrived at two o'clock this morning, tired but still in good spirits, and within a few hours were having a final rehearsal for the belated opening concert."

So far the journey had not been without casualties. While waiting at the English port for the boat to sail, one woman member of the orchestra became ill with congestion of the lungs. David Woodward, *Manchester Guardian* war correspondent, cabled home to his paper from Brussels the story of what happened then. " It was decided to send her ashore, but before a stretcher could be prepared the ship sailed, taking with her a doctor who had come out to attend to the sick player, and his two orderlies. At sea Mr. Barbirolli and members of the orchestra slept on palliasses spread on deck." Then, on the day of the concert, and during rehearsal in the Palais des Beaux Arts in Brussels, Mr. and Mrs. Barbirolli (who was to have played in an oboe concerto) both fell off the platform in the darkened concert hall. They fell into the stalls, and Mrs. Barbirolli broke her arm and was

" HOME-WORK " AT INNSBRUCK DURING THE 1948
AUSTRIAN TOUR

prevented from taking any part in the concerts. "Otherwise," another war çorrespondent wrote, "Charles Collier, the veteran of the party, who is seventy-three, and the twenty-four women members of the orchestra are standing up to the strain well."

The first concert at Brussels took place, yet another war correspondent pointed out, "as Nazi troops and tanks once more swarmed into Belgium", for Runstedt's Ardennes offensive was on. But for all that, there was a wildly enthusiastic audience of 2,500 British troops, most of them on short leave from the front. The orchestra returned later to Brussels. The same enthusiasm marked all the other concerts, the last being held in Ostend. A grand gala concert was given in Brussels on Christmas Day, and on Boxing Day the orchestra travelled to Holland to give concerts at Eindhoven and Nijmegen. It was at one of these concerts that the hall came under fire when a German plane swooped down as soldiers were leaving and machine-gunned the entrance, without, however, doing any harm to anybody.

Barbirolli pointed out on his return to England that the concerts which the orchestra gave during the tour were "precisely of the type that ought to be given in Manchester." He added: "We were determined to give the troops nothing but the best music, and the troops in turn gave us a magnificent reception. It was impossible to imagine more wonderful or appreciative audiences. They insisted on encores until sometimes the concerts ran to perhaps three-quarters of an hour beyond the planned time. After the concert members of the Forces used to gather round to talk to us."

It had been intended to give only four concerts at Eindhoven, but because of the great demand for seats the number was increased to seven. Mr. Bean said[1]: "The applause at the end of each concert was unlike any applause

[1] In the *Manchester Guardian*, January 9, 1945

the orchestra had received elsewhere. The men—many of them dirty from the front line—had no intention of letting us escape with a paltry two-hour programme. They sat immovable, demanding encore after encore, until Thomas Cheetham, the librarian, ran out of additional music. After which they came round to offer presents and give thanks for the ' experience of our lives '." For the last concert of the tour, Mr. Bean said that the Royal Theatre at Ostend was " literally crowded to the roof ". The orchestra had given seventeen concerts in fifteen days. Another casualty had been added to the list—Leonard Regan, the clarinetist, whom they left behind in Brussels Hospital. " The question now asked," wrote Mr. Bean, back in Manchester, " is ' how soon can another visit be arranged—this time nearer still to the fighting line? '."

But they were not to go abroad again until their Austrian tour in 1948.

After their return home, Barbirolli and the Hallé settled down once more to their strenuous programme of concert-giving. This continued, with but a month's holiday break for the orchestra, all the next year, and the next—going up and down the country, a week here, a week there, with an occasional flashing visit to London.

Outside this programme, Barbirolli was to find his most rewarding individual engagements in Vienna, with the Vienna Philharmonic, an orchestra which had played under such distinguished musicians as Bruno Walter and Richard Strauss, and earlier, Gustav Mahler. In Vienna, which gave Haydn, Mozart (although he was not born there), Schubert, and Johann Strauss to the world, it is still possible to find the quintessence of musical life, in spite of the things which Nazi-ism did to it.

In April 1947 a gala concert was organized by the Society for the Promotion of Cultural and Economic Relations with the Soviet Union, which Barbirolli was invited to conduct, " in honour of the anniversary of the liberation ".

The *Arbeiter Zeitung* for April 15th wrote: " John Barbirolli conducted the concert with that intensity and subdued passion which lends a work of art the power of stirring expression. His conducting reached its brilliant culminating point in the rendering of Tchaikovsky's passionate Fourth Symphony."

A week earlier Barbirolli had conducted Verdi's *Requiem* in Vienna " as a sort of finale to the mourning ceremonies of Holy Week " at the State Opera House. " John Barbirolli," wrote the *Wiener Zeitung*, " is not only a conductor with the wide and great gesture, but in the first instance the interpreter of the subtle beauties of the score." *Das Kleine Volksblatt* wrote that under Barbirolli " the brilliance and colour of the orchestral part blossomed up in the delicately sensitive *mezzo* as much as in the ardently ecstatic trio."

The *Weltepresse* wrote: " Catching fire on Verdi's genius, John Barbirolli offered us a performance which . . . can only be welcomed as a blissful present. . . . Barbirolli does not interpret: he performs."

On April 20 Barbirolli conducted *Aïda*, which sent *Das Kleine Volksblatt* into paeans of joy. " Barbirolli," the paper said, " seems born to be a conductor of opera, especially of Italian opera, as he makes its mainly musical quintessence read unencumbered orgiastic triumphs of melodious wealth under his hands. With unerring certainty he knows how to build up contrasts and climaxes; how to make the stage and orchestra conform to a remarkable degree; how to give the singer what is ' the singer's ', and to the orchestra what is ' the orchestra's ' . . . . The success of this great evening . . . lay with Barbirolli."

The *Wiener Zeitung* wrote of the same performance of

Aïda: " The complete concord of the stage and orchestra, the precise keeping of the pauses—increasing the tension —showed the work of a man completely dominating his subject."

It was the *Weltepresse* critic who had touched the secret of Barbirolli's success—his " catching fire ", not only " on Verdi's genius ", but on the musical climate of the great city. Barbirolli's mind is like a sensitive plate " of imagination all compact ", and it is this thing in him that amounts to genius. He has remained, after all these years, acutely receptive of the " feel " of things, acutely and quickly responsive to the inner significance of great occasions. He dominated Vienna's great orchestra, as he had dominated that of New York, because he so completely identified himself with it. " He does not interpret, he performs ", describes him better than most that has been written about him.

In August 1947 Barbirolli took the Hallé Orchestra to Edinburgh's successful International Festival. There was one famous critic present at one of his concerts who was in a better position to assess the qualities of the Hallé, and to compare the new with the old, than any other critic living. This was Neville Cardus, who was seeing with the eyes and hearing with the ears of a man who had been absent from this country, in Australia, for more than seven years. He went up to Edinburgh from London to write about the festival for his old paper, the *Manchester Guardian*.

He wrote of the Hallé: " Into this challenging air, broad and unbounded, came the Hallé Orchestra, and made its contribution definite and characteristic. [It was the first time Cardus had heard the reconstituted orchestra.] Visitors from overseas were incredulous that this was an ensemble of comparatively brief growth. The playing was extremely free of any suggestion of provincialism. Barbirolli's achievement in creating this orchestra has been astonishing—I had nearly said miraculous." And the opinion of Cardus was echoed in many other quarters during the festival.

The outstanding event of the first part of 1948 was the tour which Barbirolli made, this time with the entire Hallé Orchestra, in Austria, under the auspices of the British Council, in June. They were to have flown to Prague in May to represent British music at an international festival, but this visit was cancelled when the Czech regime became "Sovietized". The Austrian tour was a sensational success. It included concerts at Innsbruck, Salzburg, Graz, and Vienna, where, of course, Barbirolli himself was no stranger. The journey was made by air. It took two Dakotas to transport the baggage and musical instruments alone. Two other planes carried Mr. Barbirolli and the eighty-odd members of the orchestra, with Mr. Bean, the general manager, and one or two others of the Society's officers. Charles Collier, the principal harpist (since retired), now seventy-seven years old, would not be left behind, and a picture in the newspapers at home showed him dancing with one of the young women players at a wayside inn, as Mr. Barbirolli sat at a table looking on, enjoying their display of high spirits. The incident occurred when the orchestra's coach broke down between Salzburg and Graz. The orchestra had a wonderful reception everywhere. At one of the Vienna concerts Barbirolli took seventeen calls.

Mr. Bean wrote an account of the tour for the *Manchester Guardian*. In this he said:

"Although our journey through Austria started on the Salzburg airfield, it did not really take hold of our imaginations until some two hours later when, having passed through the grandeur of the Berchtesgaden Salient, within a few miles of Hitler's retreat, we drew up for tea in the Tyrolese village of Lofer before one of the most delightful inns imaginable outside an operetta by Johann Strauss. The host and his wife and daughter, in Tyrolese costume, stood in the street to welcome us . . . In a twinkling a meal was set before us, laid on spotless chequered tablecloths sprinkled with freshly-gathered flowers. . . ."

He then touched briefly on what seemed significant in the events of the remaining twelve days.

" There was," he says, " the journey through the valley of the Inn to Innsbruck, with its freshly-painted chalets, each with its individual carving, its gothic letters, its neatly stacked woodpile, and its array of flowers flinging their gay challenge to the impersonal hills. There were the walks around and in Innsbruck, with its medieval streets nestling in the amphitheatre of towering mountains. There was the all-too-brief return to Salzburg, where, after a triumphant concert (at which the orchestra with Evelyn Rothwell as soloist gave a performance of the newly-discovered Mozart oboe concerto from the original parts in the possession of the Mozarteum), the players could loiter in courtyards and mount staircases trod by Mozart.

"And for contrast there was the grim journey to Graz, during which, after climbing fantastic altitudes which made us long for the security of air transport, one of the coaches broke down and stranded half the orchestra in a mountain village from where they were rescued at nine in the evening by army lorries.

" Of Vienna itself memories are mixed, modulating between sadness at the senseless destructions of war and at the air of unreality behind that city's wondrous façade, and delight in the rich associations which the city must always have for the musician.

" But, vivid as all these memories are, the crowning experience of the tour was the thrill of playing to the critical and (in the words of one flattering critic) the ' spoiled ' audiences of Salzburg, Graz, Innsbruck, and Vienna. The orchestra rose to the occasion with an audacity that fully justified John Barbirolli's belief in the splendid quality of the instrument he has fashioned.

" Many of the experiences were, perhaps, too crowded to be fully savoured at the time. But recollected in tranquillity they will be bound to influence the style and affect the attitude of all who participated. Merely to have visited the houses where Beethoven, Schubert, and Brahms lived, to have walked where Mozart walked, to have gazed on the drop curtain that was raised for the first performance of The Magic Flute, or at the rostrum from which was conducted the first performance of the Fifth Symphony, is to have added something to one's power of making music. To have brought to this home of music a British orchestra with its own individual—and Mancunian—traditions, and to have been apprecated there, is a stimulus to conductor and players no less than to the city whose ambassador it has been."

The applause that followed all the orchestra's performances, long and unrestrained, left no doubt in the mind of everybody present that the Hallé's visit was a brilliant success. Apart from the purely musical aspect, it was felt that this flattering reception had great significance. It was agreed that the visit had promoted the mutual cultural interests of the two countries, and inspired a closer feeling of friendship. That, in part, had been the object of the British Council in arranging the tour. The reaction of the music critics, especially in the Viennese Press, provided some corrective to the outbursts of mass enthusiasm, and brought musical perspective to what went on in the concert halls. There is in all the Viennese Press notices a certain reserve, side by side with an eagerness not to mar the occasion with a too hypercritical assessment of the visiting orchestra.

After all, it must always be a daring venture to take any orchestra to the home of the Vienna Philharmonic. The Viennese public are rightly proud of their famous orchestra, which is steeped in a tradition that is rooted in the very essence of classical music. Of Barbirolli's quality they were already aware. They had taken him to their hearts and shown him gratitude, as no other public can, for new musical experiences. Where the two orchestras were concerned comparisons were almost inevitable, however hard the critics tried to avoid them.

The critic of the *Wiener Kurier* (June 2, 1948) said of the playing at one concert : " It is not individual virtuoso playing, but the spirit of a mature past, closely linked with Vienna through the personality of Hans Richter, which lies at the bottom of the ' goodwill ' of the Hallé orchestra . . ." Noting the link with Richter seemed a happy touch, as was the recollection by others of the fact that the orchestra had had as its founder Karl Hallé, the Westphalian. These things seemed to shed an aura around the Manchester players and their conductor, coloured as they were with what one or two critics called Barbirolli's " Italian *brio* ". There was general surprise that there were so many women in the orchestra, but no one sought to draw any musical inferences therefrom. It appeard to some vastly intriguing to find not only women violinists, 'cellists, and viola players, but great must have been the buzz of excitement to find that women players had even captured the oboe and the trombone and, greatest wonder of all, the timpani. The Vienna *Der Abend* thought the best group in the orchestra was the wind section, " with their astounding flexibility and artistic perspective ". *Die Presse* observed that the orchestra was " excellently schooled playing with great verve and tension ". Barbirolli included in his programme the C major Symphony of Mozart, which had seldom been heard, even in Vienna. In this, *Die Presse* said, Barbirolli and his orchestra "reached the balance between pleasure and inner conviction ".

Wiener Tageszeitung was impressed by the Hallé woodwind players, but thought Vienna had little to learn from the string playing, saying, " We are spoiled in that respect ". And yet there is this admission: " What has to be fully appreciated is the intensity of their way of handling the bow, right down to the last player." The programme for the concert—the second in Vienna—included Elgar's *Enigma Variations*, the Purcell suite arranged by Barbirolli, Vaughan Williams's *Fantasia on a Theme of Tallis*, the Mozart C major and Dvořák's No. 4 symphonies. Apart from Mozart, here were idioms which were less familiar to the Viennese. As might have been expected, the Press and critics at Salzburg, Innsbruck, and Graz, were less restrained. The *Salzburger Nachrichten* said of the Hallé: " They are an excellently disciplined orchestral unit, whose precision proves that each of its members is an eminent artist ", and that Ravel's *Daphnis and Chloe* gave the orchestra " full opportunity to show their artistic perfection ". Of Elgar's *Enigma*, the *Nachrichten* observed: " His [Elgar's] love of splendour and grandeur, his pathos, his lack of simplicity, give his music too much the stamp of the day, and make it somewhat faded." Dr. Albert Riester, in the *Tiroler Tageszeitung*, wrote praising the orchestra and its conductor, in an article headed, " A wizard of the orchestra ", which ended with the words: " For several minutes the house, packed to the roof, resounded with such enthusiastic applause for John Barbirolli and his orchestra as Innsbruck has seldom known ". *Graz am Abend* (*Weltpresse*) rose to heights of lyrical praise in saying: " This wizard conductor, whose profile recalls that of Caruso, is characterized by inflexible will, passionate precision, and faculty for penetrating any composition, and a vivacity instantly imparting itself to the orchestra and the public . . . sparing in his movements, guiding rather with his intuitively controlling eyes. How carefully, without the aid of a baton, he models with a sculptor's hand the andante of Mozart's crystal clear Symphony No. 34. What a choreographic touch he imparts to the trio in Dvořák's gorgeous Fourth; what electrifying vitality to its finale." The paper adds: " Richard Strauss's adage that ' only he who has conducted the Philharmonic Orchestra can know what it means ', can also be applied to the Hallé Orchestra, with its classical precision and its famous violas, which may well be called unique. . . . The audience were carried off their feet." On that note the tour continued until the end.

The Viennese and provincial critics were again high in their praise of Barbirolli himself, confirming previous impressions which have already been noted. But, as being typical, let Dr. Riester speak again: " John Barbirolli," he wrote, " is a man of true dignity, devoid of jarring mannerisms, a genuine cosmopolitan of art. His incantations are often no more than a breath, yet they are apt to assume the power of a palpitating lung, the driving-power of the whole enterprise. His rhythmic energy . . . and great clarity of thought as expressed in a profound understanding of the beauty of the cantilena, merit as much unstinted admiration as his invariable respect for the genius of the composition."

Again in August 1948, Barbirolli and the Hallé gave performances at the Edinburgh Festival. The first concert followed a performance the previous day by the Huddersfield Choir and the Liverpool orchestra under Sargent of Brahms' B minor Mass. Earlier still the Concertgebouw Orchestra from Amsterdam had given a series of concerts. The Hallé's playing made a tremendous impression. Of the first concert, The Times critic wrote: " Not Amurath an Amurath succeeds, but Hallé, the Liverpool Philharmonic Orchestra. The orchestra from Manchester gave the first of its two concerts in the Usher Hall last night under the direction of Mr. Barbirolli, and in a programme that included every style of orchestral music proved itself a body capable of standing comparison with any orchestra from abroad.

" The consistently beautiful quality of the string-tone, brilliant in *fortissimo* and never thin or wavering in the softest passages, was displayed at the outset.

" Of the Sibelius the orchestra gave the finest performance it has been my good fortune to hear. Everything was right— *tempo*, balance, expression. The nice adjustment of all these things is particularly difficult in this symphony. To take a particular point, the great climax, which is apt to become a roar of brazen noise, was built up with a marvellous sense of timing and, because every player was attacking his note cleanly and exactly, the texture was as limpid and as glowing with rich colour as it is possible to imagine."

Then came Ernest Newman, the great critic who prefers to call himself " Musicologist " and usually abhors festivals. Writing in the *Sunday Times* of September 5th, he said:

" For all our disappointments and annoyances at some of the earlier concerts we had full compensation in that of the Hallé Orchestra under John Barbirolli on Monday. I had not heard Mr. Barbirolli for, I think, some twenty years. He has developed into a conductor of the international front rank, and has made the present Manchester orchestra an instrument of exceptional sensitivity and polish. The whole programme—an Elizabethan suite, the Haffner Symphony, Villa Lobos's brilliantly coloured *Discrobimento do Brazil*, Stravinsky's neatly artificial Concerto in D for strings, and the Sibelius No. 5—was beautifully played.

" Of the Sibelius I do not hope ever to hear a more splendidly convincing performance. It was an inexpressible pleasure to see, for once, a great work gradually taking shape in performance as it must have done in the mind of its creator, developing steadily, logically, from acorn to mighty oak, and treated respectfully as something existing in its own right, instead of being made a mere vehicle for ' conductor's effects ' and Flash-Harry trash of that sort."

Newman began his notice with some unkind references to the Amsterdam orchestra. He wrote:

" During performances of a Handel suite and a Mozart symphony by the Concertgebouw Orchestra under Charles Münch, I could only ask myself in blank amazement why it was thought necessary to bring an orchestra all the way from Amsterdam and a conductor all the way from Paris to give us playing of such flat-footed mediocrity as this, and why anyone in his senses should travel all the way from London to Edinburgh to listen to it."

Others thought better—much better—of the Concertgebouw. It takes all sorts of critics to make a musical world.

CHAPTER XVI

HIGH HOPES FOR THE FUTURE

THE time has come to focus Barbirolli against the background built up in previous chapters—the portrait needs rounding off. And yet a portrait is not enough: you cannot see what lies behind, for a portrait is too static, and Barbirolli is anything but static. For one of the most impressive things about him is his sheer mobility, combined with inexhaustible energy. The longest journeys have not tired him.* He has conducted a score of concerts in as many days, each in a different city, travelling from one end of Britain or America to the other in the course of them, and finishing up fresh. He seems to have found the secret of conserving his strength. He has not spared himself during rehearsals and performances, and yet he has never lost his mental or physical poise. At the end of a great concert, which would have left many another conductor limp, he has always been ready to make a speech or indulge in private music-making at his home, or start out on a long rail or road journey. If he has complained at all of a too-crowded pro-gramme, it has always been on his players' behalf, not on his own. He realizes they have not his staying power. By the time they are "all-in " he himself has always some strength left in reserve. Barbirolli has, of course, had long vacations —longer in America than in this country. But he has never refused invitations to conduct for orchestras other than his

* He was, unfortunately, involved in a motor car accident late at night when returning to Manchester from a concert tour in the West of England in September 1948.

own during his holidays. An instance of that was when, at the end of the New York season in May 1940, he travelled to Vancouver, and after that to Chicago and down to Hollywood, to fulfil eighteen " holiday " engagements. He was then not yet forty and had strength and resilience to spare, but he has undertaken even more strenuous courses since his return to England. Seven years after that holiday tour in Canada and the U.S. in 1940, we find him, in the midst of conducting a series of over two hundred Hallé concerts in all parts of Britain, rushing off to Salzburg, Vienna, Copenhagen, and London, to take charge of other great orchestras. From each journey he gets an experience. He looks about him, comes back rich in impressions and anecdotes. Each day is a new day. Each task is a new task, even if it is no more than rehearsing and performing the same works for the thousandth time.

The remarkable thing about Barbirolli's rise to preeminence is that people have been prepared to entrust him with the highest musical posts on the strength of first impressions or on only slight acquaintance. The words " dynamic " and " Napoleonic ", if loosely used in the context of newspaper stories and gossip about him, would not be very far wide of the mark in any objective estimate of his personality, his breadth of vision, and his methods of mastering and then presenting the great musical classics. Nor has such language been used about him by laymen only. There is hardly any profession in the world more given to mutual denigration than the musical profession. A few years ago one London conductor in all seriousness told the present writer that another London conductor, who was, and still is, something of a world figure, " could not read a full score " and that for that reason he never used one when conducting. This allegation was patently absurd. For one thing it completely ignored the fact, which the man who made it knew as well as any one, that the conductor thus maligned had conducted some of the world's leading orchestras, not only in the performance of classics, but also in unfamiliar modern works, and he had been acclaimed for the brilliance of his interpretations. The allegation also overlooked the great amount of work which every conductor has to do in the rehearsal room, in the course of which any ignorance of the score would at once make itself apparent and would have a damaging effect on the future relations between orchestra and conductor.

That example in denigration is a mild one compared with some of the things which some musicians, and those not among the smaller fry, say about some other musicians. Perhaps this need not be stressed, except to make the point that a musician has to be unquestionably good to be accepted as an outstanding figure among other musicians.

In studying a man like Barbirolli it is by no means easy to come at the human stuff that lies behind his public appearance. It was Browning who said that every man has two sides—one he shows to the world and the other to those he loves and by whom he is beloved. A conductor, who must be a creative artist in the sense that he gathers up all the elements of a musical work and of its means of expression, and gives form and shape to performance, cannot afford to give too much of himself to social activities. In most cases his private life is of the simplest—that is if he is fortunate enough to have a private life. There are, however, times when a quiet evening at his home becomes a sheer necessity to his peace of mind and physical health, even if he spends it reading scores or talking to a friend or two about music. Barbirolli reads the newspapers and his favourite books. And he will occasionally go to see a film and gets much enjoyment from it, even if he cannot help thinking what a fine concert hall the cinema would make!

To an audience, perhaps, Barbirolli may seem a lonely figure with a burden. But Barbirolli is never lonely in the sense that he remains on his pinnacle, aloof from his players or his immediate circle of friends. Elgar went to the races, and Barbirolli has played his cricket, which taught him patience and gave him staying power. He will often take his ease in a pub or hotel bar during a break in rehearsal or after a concert, or chat with his players in the train or the motor coach as they travel up and down the country. And he can do this without lessening his authority in the smallest degree. At next day's rehearsal he will still be able to terrify them with a look. From his own experience as an orchestral player he can enter into their mental world and help them to bear the occasional tedium of concert giving.

Rehearsals, governed as to frequency and duration by the rules of the Musician's Union, see him at his best, and no one works harder. He was staggered when a well-known conductor in London once told him that he was presenting a programme which he had not rehearsed with the orchestra. Such a thing seemed incredible to the man who is universally acknowledged to be perhaps the finest and most exacting orchestra-trainer in the world.

Indeed, Barbirolli would not be what he is or where he is to-day if he had not insisted on the most exhaustive rehearsal, in detail and all together, of every work. He made up his mind firmly about that from the moment when, still in his twenties, he became conductor of the British National Opera Company. It is in the rehearsal room that he gets down to the serious business of studying the works to be played, studying them bar by bar and studying them whole. It is then, too, that he is able to give his players the benefit of his own studies and of his vast experience, and decide the pattern of the performance. This is when those dazzling performances which hold an audience spellbound are made, although the audience may not know it. Even so, between the final rehearsal and what happens in the concert hall, there is always the human element in the orchestra which is liable to undo the good work done in the rehearsal room, unless the conductor himself remains alert and freshly vital and can communicate his vitality to the orchestra and keep them at the same pitch until the last note of the concert. This is a strain which the conductor must bear alone. Barbirolli, like most great conductors, has his mannerisms—the digging plunging motion of the left hand, the leaning forward and screwing up his face into a frightening scowl. None uses his hands more eloquently. Every nerve in them seems vibrant with music. Some find him " just a little theatrical ". Maybe it is the Italian in him. Yet every gesture, every flourish has its meaning and has its purpose. He is not in the least a showman, and he does not know what it means to " play to the gallery ".

As an American writer said of him: " He has the great gift of persuading his audiences not only to listen to music, but to share his own joy and spiritual satisfaction in its re-creation."

A year or so ago, when the Hallé Orchestra gave one of their periodical concerts in London at the Royal Albert Hall, the music critic of The Times took Barbirolli to task for what he described as his " incalculable beat ". E. J. Moeran, the composer, a few days later in a letter to the Editor of The Times, attacked the critic with some heat, contending that a conductor of genius is to a great extent a law unto himself, cannot be confined within academic rules, and must keep his style fluid so that it adapts itself to the emotional and artistic needs of the performance. Moeran had little difficulty in refuting the critic, because the justification of Barbirolli's methods lay in the admitted brilliance of the performance itself.

Barbirolli may be elastic in his style and even incalculable to the critic sitting in the stalls and later pondering the matter in his newspaper office, but no one has yet been able to impugn his musical integrity. As another writer has said: " Integrity is the core of Barbirolli's musical being and it has always kept him from any effort to exploit himself at the expense of the art he serves. He has never wooed the flamboyant conductorial tricks . . . or catered for sensation-seekers by indulging in temperamental outbursts."

Barbirolli's success has had the effect on him of an unexpected, grand and expensive present. Rather than being a reason for vainglory, he has accepted it as a kind of homage to the geniuses dead and gone, of whose masterpieces he is but the humble interpreter. The triumph has been theirs, not his. The glory is reflected from Beethoven, Mozart, Bach, Brahms, and all the rest of the masters who cannot now claim it for themselves. In this respect he finds himself in the company of such men as Toscanini, Furtwangler, Bruno Walter, and a few others.

And yet Barbirolli, as an interpreter with shining gifts, would be justified in claiming credit in his own right, in so far as his performances excelled those of others. And if he should tell you that on his last visit to the Austrian capital, the Vienna Philharmonic Orchestra " fell for him " and that the applause was tremendous, that would be to state a fact; and because he thinks that you, being a friend of his, would like to know (which you do), whether his visit was a success. But he will add with even greater pleasure that it has been the members of the orchestra themselves, who had invited him to conduct them. To him that is the final proof that they regard him as a " musician's musician ", not because things are easier for them when he is there, but because he can combine their individual efforts into a vital ensemble that wrings the very heart from the music.

Barbirolli has given his views from time to time on the art of conducting to newspaper men in America and to "listening clubs" in this country. They are interesting expositions of the thing, and its toil and sweat, but about the greatest secret of all he is silent. What is it that makes an orchestra play better under one conductor than under another?

This is not a thing observed by listeners alone. It is the experience of orchestral players themselves. It is not easy to describe the essence of a conductor's power. It does not lie only in his beat or his knowledge of the score. This incommunicable something is a compound of many qualities, among them musicianship, personality, inexhaustible physical and nervous energy, acute sensibility, imagination, a sense of style, and a complete surrender of the ego to the spirit of the music. Of these ingredients, probably the greatest and most essential are personality, inexhaustible energy, a sense of style, and the complete surrender. And it would not be too much to say that Barbirolli has them all in full measure.

Besides the question of the qualities which go to the making of a great conductor, there is the correlated one of how his fame becomes established among his own generation. Arnold Bennett once propounded a rough and ready test suggested by newspaper contents bills and headlines. He maintained that fame was reached in three stages and mentioned what happened when, for instance, a peer of the realm died. If the name of the peer is not generally known the newspaper bill will announce simply: " Peer dead." As the degree of fame increased it would read: " Well-known peer dead," then " Lord Muggleton dead," and finally (and this is fame), " Muggleton dead ".

But, of course, this test tells you nothing of how the transition from obscurity to fame takes place, nor does the mere recital of the man's achievements in the newspaper report itself.

Fame represents an attitude of mind towards any individual among his contemporaries, their reaction to the public expression of his ego. In the case of an orchestral conductor it is a comparatively ephemeral thing. Nothing he creates lives after him except his reputation, and that merely in the form of a passing reference or two in print, or a drawing-room reminiscence.

This is also true of executive musicians famous in their day. Who can say that in another generation the name of Paderewski will not have been forgotten, save among musical historians and people who still possess his gramophone records? And even then, there will be little to determine his exact contribution to the music of his time. The only immortals are composers.

None the less a brilliant conductor, if he lasts long enough, will have brought a succession of wonderful experiences to his audiences, as well as to the orchestras he has conducted. This can only be measured in terms of pure happiness—of the immeasurable. An electrifying performance of a noble work of music like Beethoven's "Eroica" symphony or Verdi's "Requiem" may linger for years in the memory of those who heard it and will always be associated by a discriminating listener with the conductor.

That is the conductor's nearest approach to the threshold of posterity. Beyond that his reward is the supreme satisfaction of having achieved performances as nearly perfect as man can make them. From each such achievement he springs to yet higher standards, by virtue of which he leaves the impress of his personality and interpretative genius upon an ever-widening concourse of the public.

Barbirolli was still in his early twenties when he first caught the eye of those who were in a position to place opportunities in his way. He found himself promoted overnight from the orchestra to the rostrum, because there was one man with enough vision and discernment to realize that the young 'cello player had the mark of a leader upon him, a certain intensity of style and an enormous power of concentration. He had gone through the Royal Academy of Music and Trinity College of Music and so far had travelled by the hardest road. But so had many of his orchestral colleagues. And it was just that unmistakable but indefinable something that raised him out of the orchestra pit, that came in time to place him head and shoulders above his contemporaries in the ranks of conductors.

He has never uttered carefully premeditated and polished witticisms that might be quoted by newspaper columnists or society hostesses. He has always refused to become anything like a " social lion ". He has been too busy and too wrapped up in music to seek popularity in that way. He has never exploited himself, as other conductors have exploited themselves. Such publicity as he has had has been won purely on the strength of his musical attainments, and even hard-boiled professional critics confess to having been as thrilled by these as the rawest listener.

His name—which in itself has a certain magical euphony and rhythm and sounds familiar at first hearing—began to appear often in the newspapers, ascending the scale of fame and shedding prefixes, as in the case of Arnold Bennett's peer. It appeared in large letters on the hoardings in posters announcing concerts and opera. It was bandied about in foyers and other places where musicians and music-lovers foregather. As his career unfolded, rocketing suddenly to some new height, it was sufficient for his surname to appear in a headline for it to tell almost all that was known about him. The name came to mean something out of the ordinary in the way of music: it held for the concert-goer or opera-lover the promise of a world of delight, of an authentic musical experience.

Like every other conductor of note Barbirolli has all the time had to consider limiting factors, chief among them being the calibre and resources of his orchestras and the musical intelligence and taste of his audience. But only a few of living conductors have his power of lifting a whole performance and its atmosphere from a mediocre to a vital and exciting level.

Another limiting factor is his responsibility, which he has always taken seriously, towards unknown or rising contemporary composers. As the arbiter of his own programmes, he has never resisted their claims to be heard. He has realized that it rests with the musical directors of the world's leading orchestras whether a new composer's work shall live or not, or even obtain a hearing at all.

He has divested himself completely of all prejudice, nor has he waited for a new work to become established in other conductors' repertoires before taking it up himself. Indeed, especially in America, he has laid himself open to criticism by including works by little-known British, as well as American composers.

The programme for his opening concert in Carnegie Hall with the New York Philharmonic Symphony Orchestra in November 1936, it may be recalled, included Bax's *The Tale the Pine Trees Knew*, which is not often played even in the composer's own country. It was characteristic of Barbirolli that he refused to " play safe " merely to make his own success secure, although, heaven knows, he would have been pardoned if he had done so, at this, his début in America's musical capital. In the event the Bax work was received by the critics somewhat coolly and probably with reserve by an audience fed on the classics, but this did not discourage him from continuing to present modern works whose intrinsic merits seemed to him to demand a hearing and to preserve a balance in his programmes as between classics and moderns.

And if in that first programme there was the Bax work, there was also the *Second Brahms Symphony*, and that made up for everything.

If Barbirolli prides himself on one thing it is the catholicity of his musical taste, and his open-mindedness. This is rare among conductors. Too often the guiding principle in their programme building is: "What do I like?" or "What work would best enhance my reputation?"

Some conductors make no secret of their strong likes and dislikes. For this reason their performances are apt to become stereotyped and unsatisfactory. Few can afford to omit from their programmes certain works, however much they dislike them, and just to the extent that they dislike them, the works suffer.

And what of Barbirolli the musician? We have seen that the groundwork of his knowledge and craft was the 'cello, taken up to "make me sit still". That early restlessness had to be disciplined and canalized in purely musical achievement. Healthy outdoor impulses of boyhood had to be sublimated in the sedentary job of making a musician of him.

But still the problem of an outlet for his superabundant energy remained—"I always wanted to conduct," Barbirolli once told a friend. But the distance between a 'cello player and a conductor is heavens-wide. An instrumentalist, besides playing his instrument, is concerned only with its literature and the part allotted to it in an orchestral or quartet score. Most instrumentalists are content with that. If they all tried to be virtuoso soloists there would be no orchestras.

As a 'cellist Barbirolli might have gone a long way. Who can tell? As it happened, he "wanted to conduct", and in the end the larger field claimed him. He did not shirk its responsibilities or its demands on his energy and mental powers.

A conductor must know as much as it is possible to know in a life-time of all forms of music—operatic, symphony, choral, piano, violin, 'cello, vocal, woodwind, and brass. Not only that, but he must be familiar with every established work in the operatic and orchestral repertoire. He is bound to engage in endless research. To enter the composer's mind, he must know all about the composer, how he lived and worked, what were the musical ideas that resulted in the texture of his music, what were his ideas and methods of orchestration.

The conductor must allow for the fact that orchestral instruments have constantly been modified and improved since the composer's day, giving better tone and allowing for greater volume and speed. Also, orchestras are much bigger than they were in the days of the classical composers, and produce effects far beyond those visualized or " auralized " by the composers themselves. Knowledge of these important factors must be gained by the conductor before he decides what interpretation or " reading " to give to a particular classic.

But a *pianissimo* is always a *pianissimo*, whether an orchestra has thirty or a hundred players. And the composer's markings and directions in general stand, or should stand, for all time and under all conditions. Yet as everybody knows there is often room for a variation in the *tempo* as originally conceived here, or the introduction of a *rubato* there. But these are departures which will only be forgiven an experienced conductor who has first and all the time, the interests of the music at heart.

Barbirolli has seldom been accused of taking unwarrantable liberties with a music score, although his " readings " and *tempi* have sometimes caused differences among critics sitting with scores in their hands. If he has drawn out a phrase or thrown in a new accent occasionally, it was because he has thought the artistic effect of the work would be enhanced by it rather than because he wanted to give a " reading" different from that of another conductor. We have stressed all through this book that Barbirolli's musical integrity has remained unassailable throughout his career.

The writer recalls one of Barbirolli's rehearsals in Manchester a year or two ago. His manner was one of benevolent despotism. He would go back over certain passages over and over again. He would say " It must go like this " and hum it, louder and louder, and then say, " Now, back to section K ". When he was satisfied he would grunt.

At one stage the orchestra had played through nearly half of the first movement of a symphony, when the whole company was startled by a long-drawn-out shout from the conductor—the shout consisted of one word only—" WH-A-T? " —a question, uttered as though he could not believe his ears. The players knew what he meant, and looked down, ashamed. He gazed at them sadly for a moment as though asking " How *could* you? " They played the whole movement again—perfectly.

It is thus that Barbirolli endears himself to his players. With a look he can make them feel ashamed of the smallest lapse. The conductor of a great orchestra always has the problem before him of dispensing with the services of experienced players who have grown stale or infirm in the service of the orchestra or lowering the artistic standard by keeping them on.

This problem, when Barbirolli succeeded Toscanini, proved not to be a serious one, because the orchestra, so far as personnel was concerned, was at the point to which the

Maestro himself had brought it. Consequently there was no reason for ruthless firings.

Nor was Barbirolli to be bothered by it in the case of the Hallé. The problem there was not one of firing but of hiring —and hiring wholesale. Here the position as Barbirolli found it on going to New York was reversed.

In America he, a young stranger, had to face the country's greatest orchestra, which had already had a long line of world-famous conductors. In Manchester, a collection mostly of raw, untried musicians met for the first time a world-famous conductor with whom they were to work. They soon lost their feeling of strangeness and their initial fright under his kindly, if weighty, touch. They knew he could make an orchestra out of them, raw as they were, an orchestra to which it would be an honour to belong. If they had not had it already, they were to marvel how thoroughly he could give them a pride in their work, a sense of vocation, even as he felt these things himself.

It did not take Barbirolli long to re-establish his reputation at home. All he had to do was to superimpose that which he had gained in New York upon the estimate that had been formed of him by his countrymen before he left for America in 1936. This had never happened before in the case of a British conductor. When he arrived home Britain was recovering from the desperate position in which she had found herself after Dunkirk. America had come into the war, considerably easing the tension in Britain.

As we have seen, Barbirolli had always been prepared to do his share of the fighting. But wisdom prevailed. With a gun in his hand, his contribution to the national effort would have been negligible. With a baton, he helped to uplift the national spirit. As the conductor of a great orchestra he was as indispensable to the continuance of Britain's community life as a Cabinet Minister.

Even so, he would not have accepted this rôle with the same readiness if he had not been given the opportunity to meet the musical needs of the men and women in uniforms or overalls. Around Manchester, from 1943 onwards until the end of the war, thousands of the American Forces were stationed. Among them were a large number of men and women who had regularly attended his concerts in Carnegie Hall. Many of them approached him personally and he shook them by the hand and chatted with them about their home town.

Back in England, he has been perhaps more accessible than most of our conductors, apart from mere autograph-hunters. The American idiom has always amused Barbirolli, although he did not permit himself to acquire even a trace of it.

His English is correct, even formal. He seldom uses slang. But he could laugh at one American soldier who re-called in Manchester that he heard a " dame playing a bull fiddle " (the double-bass) in an orchestra "back home ". It must have been at Toledo, Ohio, or some other of the smaller American cities Barbirolli had visited.

If Barbirolli has ever conceived of himself as having a "mission ", it would be that of bringing the wonder and beauty of the great classical and modern musical master-pieces into the lives of the masses. He has often described this as one of his chief aims. There is no cant about it, and he means it.

A Chicago musical journalist already quoted referred to him as " this aristocrat ". He would repudiate the title.

It is to the masses that he warms most. They remind him of his mission. The Sunday afternoon audiences at Belle Vue consist mostly of young people, students, bank clerks, working men and girls, typists. He has said that he would rather play to such an audience than to any collection of social dowagers and their family satellites that used to pack Carnegie Hall.

There is in the infectious and unrestrained enthusiasm of the Belle Vue audiences a quality which has struck observers as being peculiar to these concerts. Pau Casals, when he played there, told Barbirolli that he had felt it at once. It is part of the atmosphere which Barbirolli himself has created.

The concerts are supposed to be more popular than the mid-week subscription concerts in Peter Street. " Popular " in Manchester means an all-Beethoven programme, and not Viennese waltzes. Many critics, indeed, have found the musical taste all over the North far more advanced than it is in London.

Barbirolli has become firmly established in the affections of his regular audiences. They miss him when he is away, and give him a frenzied ovation when he returns. To him this is worth all the laurels he won in New York. It shows him that his " mission " is succeeding. At the same time he is educating his public, leading it towards the less severely classical—the less familiar. He knows he has it in his power to shape its musical life according to his own pattern. He can give to its musical taste the something of his own integrity. He enjoys himself.

Four of his players, led by Laurance Turner, the leader of the Hallé orchestra, recently arranged to play quartets to an audience in a town outside Manchester, when the cellist fell ill. Barbirolli took his place and played under his own leader. On that occasion, too, Barbirolli enjoyed himself. If it had been thirty-five years ago he would have earned five shillings. That—is it not?—is the true musical life. Barbirolli was a musician before he became a conductor. He is still a musician, in love with his instrument.

During the last few years Barbirolli, by arrangement with

the Hallé Society, has undertaken many conducting engagements abroad. There have been the visits to Salzburg and Vienna. He conducted opera with the Sadler's Wells Company in Hamburg. On the invitation of the French Government he went over to Paris to conduct the Paris Conservatoire Orchestra, the third oldest in the world (coming next to Vienna and New York).

Especially in Vienna has he made a profound impression. The critiques in the Viennese Press, packed audiences, and the applause of both the orchestra and audiences, testified to it. These experiences have been useful, perhaps, in checking any tendency in his musical horizon to contract. Also Barbirolli enjoys travel, enjoys new horizons. That is why he can stand so much of it." *

While he is away guest conductors take his place with the Hallé. These have included Nikolai Malko, who came over from the U.S.A., as did Bernard Herrmann, to whose *Moby Dick* cantata Barbirolli gave its first performance in New York. Enrique Jorda, a young conductor from Madrid, has conducted the Hallé in a series of concerts two years running. Josef Krips, the conductor of the Vienna State Opera, came over to conduct the Hallé during Barbirolli's absence in Vienna.

These interchanges, again, have been good for the Hallé audiences. They have given them a sense of the international character of the orchestra they so loyally support and enabled them to enjoy different styles of conducting. They have also widened the orchestral players' experience.

Barbirolli could, in fact, claim that his orchestra, although based on Manchester, is an international one. He has cherished the ambition of taking it to the United States, and

---

* Since this was written it has been announced that Barbirolli is to conduct the Berlin Philharmonic Orchestra and to undertake a tour in South Africa.

has told Manchester, " Look what an advertisement for your city such a tour would be! "

In spite of a good deal of frustration in his plans for the orchestra, Barbirolli makes no public complaint. He was asked for his ideas about the restoration of the Free Trade Hall and gave them, travelling to one or two other cities with the Manchester City Architect to collect data. At the time of writing plans which were drawn up by the corporation's draughtsmen two years or more ago rest in the pigeon holes in the City Architect's Office.

And what of the future? Barbirolli is still one of the youngest conductors of international rank. In another ten years he will still be at his prime. Sixty is no great age in a conductor. Bruno Walter is active at seventy. Toscanini is much older than that. If he should ever consider his position again, as he did when the offer from the London Symphony Orchestra was made to him in 1944, Barbirolli has several important factors to guide him to a decision. He loves his London. It was his boyhood home and the scene of his earliest successes. And yet, since Hallé could live and work in Manchester for forty years, Richter for eleven, and Harty for longer than that, there would seem always some powerful reason for staying.

In Manchester such a man as Barbirolli can build up an impregnable position. He can introduce a " Golden Age " even more memorable than Richter's. And as with Barbirolli music is all, the place which offers him a more satisfying life musically will have the greater pull. Already the Hallé is being spoken of as Britain's " premier orchestra ". If it is not that yet, it may soon become so. The comparison between what it is now and what it was in 1943 should be remembered.

There is, in fact, no comparison. But the *difference* is the measure of Barbirolli's achievement. Four concerts a week —and rehearsals—year in and year out, seeing for the most part the same faces all the time. Who would not find this slightly monotonous? It takes a big man not to feel weary of such a routine, not to let it become a routine.

"Not to let it become a routine." That is probably the secret of Barbirolli's immense energy—and patience. It explains the "freshness" of every concert Barbirolli conducts, and why the same old masterpiece sounds like a new masterpiece. All this springs from some vital force deep in the man's being, of which he may not be fully aware himself.